# READING

## Grade 1

## Table of Contents

Columbus, Ohio

**Credits:**
**McGraw-Hill Children's Publishing Editorial/Production Team**
Vincent F. Douglas, B.S. and M. Ed.
Tracey E. Dils
Jennifer Blashkiw Pawley
Teresa A. Domnauer
Tracy R. Paulus
Suzanne M. Diehm

**Big Tuna Trading Company Art/Editorial/Production Team**
Mercer Mayer
John R. Sansevere
Erica Farber
Brian MacMullen
Matthew Rossetti
Billy Steers
Diane Dubreuil
**Atomic Age, Inc.**

Send all inquiries to: McGraw-Hill Children's Publishing, 8787 Orion Place, Columbus OH 43240-4027

1-57768-811-2 7 8 9 10 VHG 05 04 03

The McGraw-Hill Companies

WELCOME TO CRITTERVILLE!
Spider
Frog
Grasshopper
Mouse
Little Critter
Little Sister
Dad
Kitty
Mom
Dog
Gator
Bat Child
Gabby
Bun Bun
Tiger
Maurice
Molly
Malcolm

# The New Puppy

Little Critter has a new puppy.

Little Critter loves the puppy.

The puppy loves Little Critter.

They are happy.

**Blends (1):** Review the sound of the blend **gr**. Have your child name each picture, then write **gr** below each picture whose name begins with the **gr** sound. Have your child put an X directly on the picture that does not begin with the **gr** sound.
**Short Vowels (2-7):** Have your child name each picture and listen to the vowel sound, then circle the correct vowel below the picture.
**Sequence (8):** Have your child look at all three pictures, then write **1** below the event that would happen first, **2** below the event that would happen second, and **3** below the event that would happen third.

# Playful Puppy

The puppy is cute.

He is small. He is brown and white.

The puppy likes to play.
The puppy likes to run.

The puppy likes to tug.

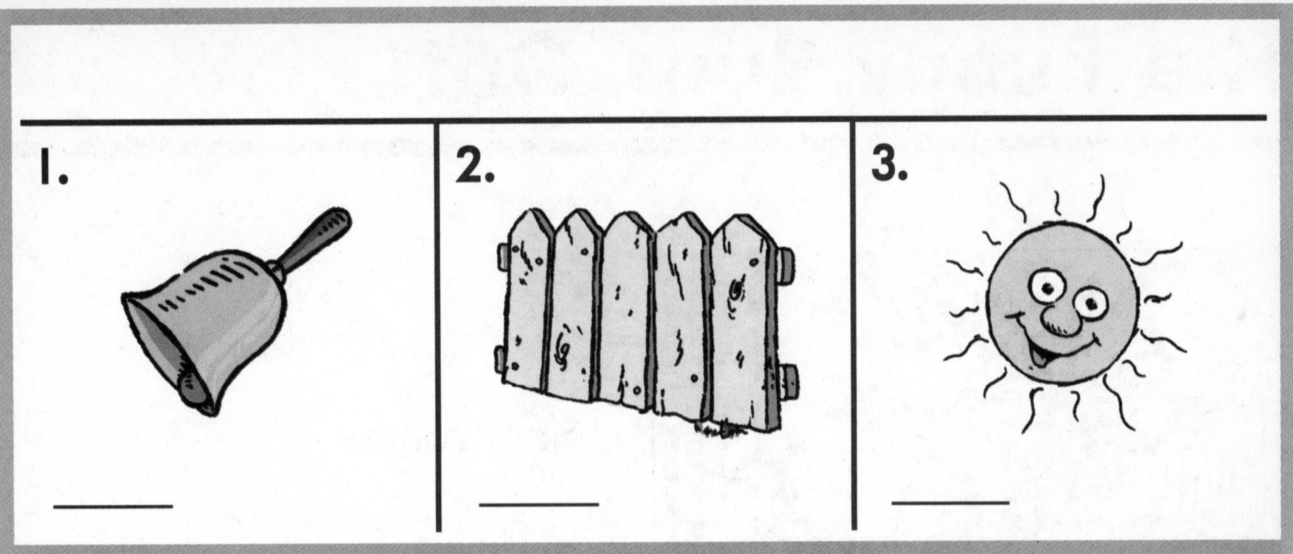

**Initial Consonants (1-3):** Have your child name each picture, listen to the beginning sound, and write the beginning letter below the picture.
**Blends (4):** Review the sound of the blend **pr**. Have your child name each picture, then write **pr** below each picture whose name begins with the **pr** sound. Have your child put an **X** directly on the picture that does not begin with the **pr** sound.
**Picture Clues (5-6):** Ask your child to read the words in each box and circle the word that best describes where the puppy is.

# The Puppy Runs Out

Mom comes in.

The puppy runs out.

Look at the puppy go!
Get the puppy!

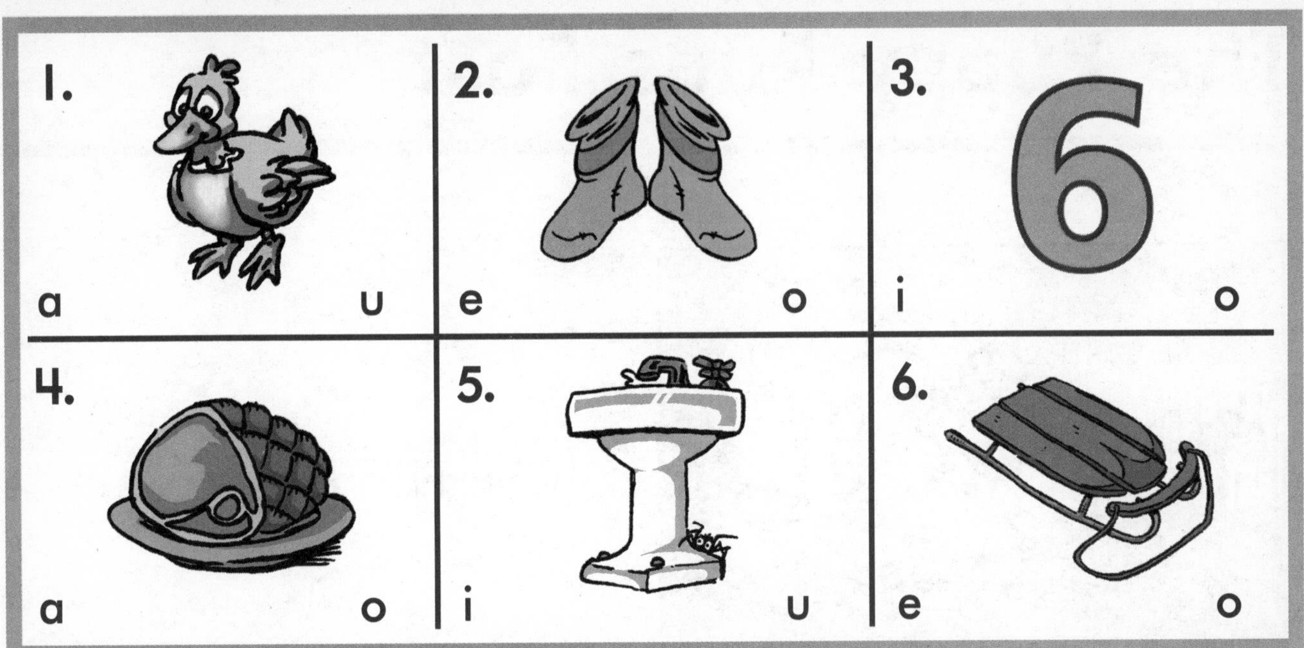


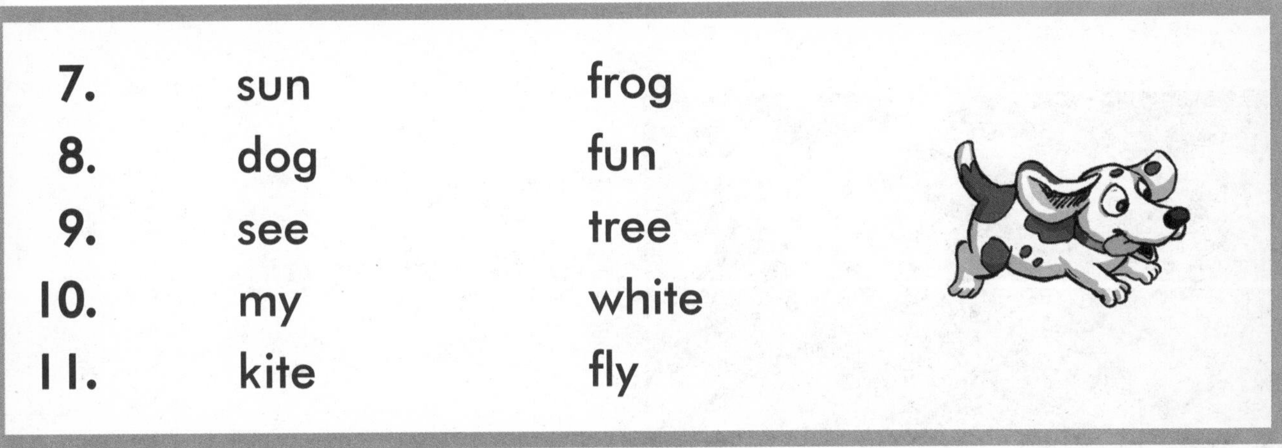


12. The puppy ran ________________.

up out in

13. ________________________ came in.

Little Critter The puppy Mom

**Short Vowels (1-6):** Have your child name each picture and listen to the vowel sound, then circle the correct vowel below the picture.
**Rhyming Words (7-11):** Have your child read the words and then draw lines to connect the words that rhyme.
**Context Clues (12-13):** Have your child read each sentence and circle the word that best completes the sentence, then write the word in the blank.

# The Puppy Runs Fast

The puppy runs.

Little Critter runs.

The puppy runs fast!
Little Critter cannot get him.
"Help!" says Little Critter.

**Initial Consonants (1-3):** Have your child name each picture, listen to the beginning sound, and write the beginning letter below the picture.
**Final Consonants (4-6):** Have your child name each picture, listen to the ending sound, and write the ending letter below the picture.
**Picture Clues (7-8):** Ask your child to read the sentences in each box and circle the sentence that best describes the picture.

# Little Sister Helps

“I will help!” says Little Sister.

Little Sister and Little Critter run. The puppy runs and runs!

The puppy runs faster. They cannot get him.

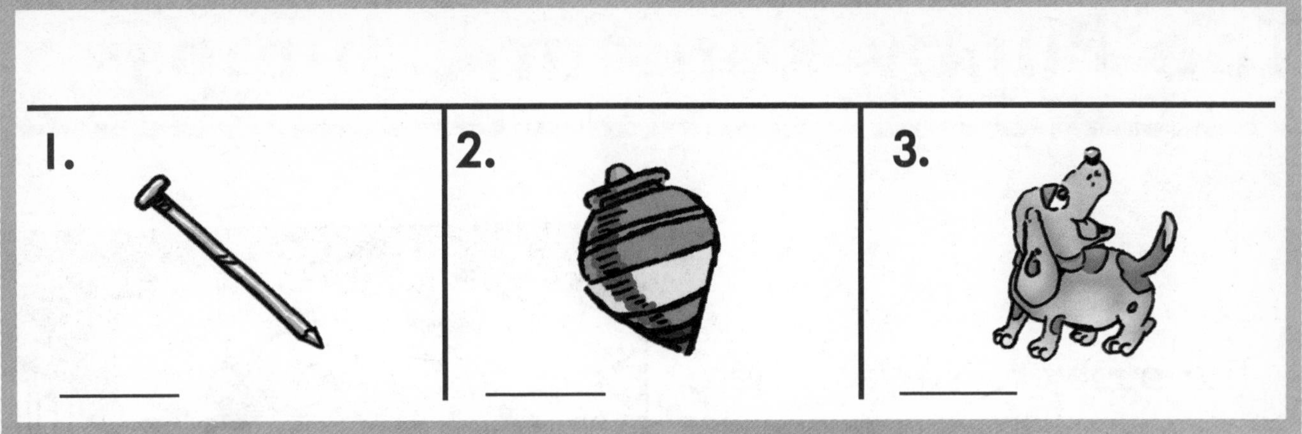


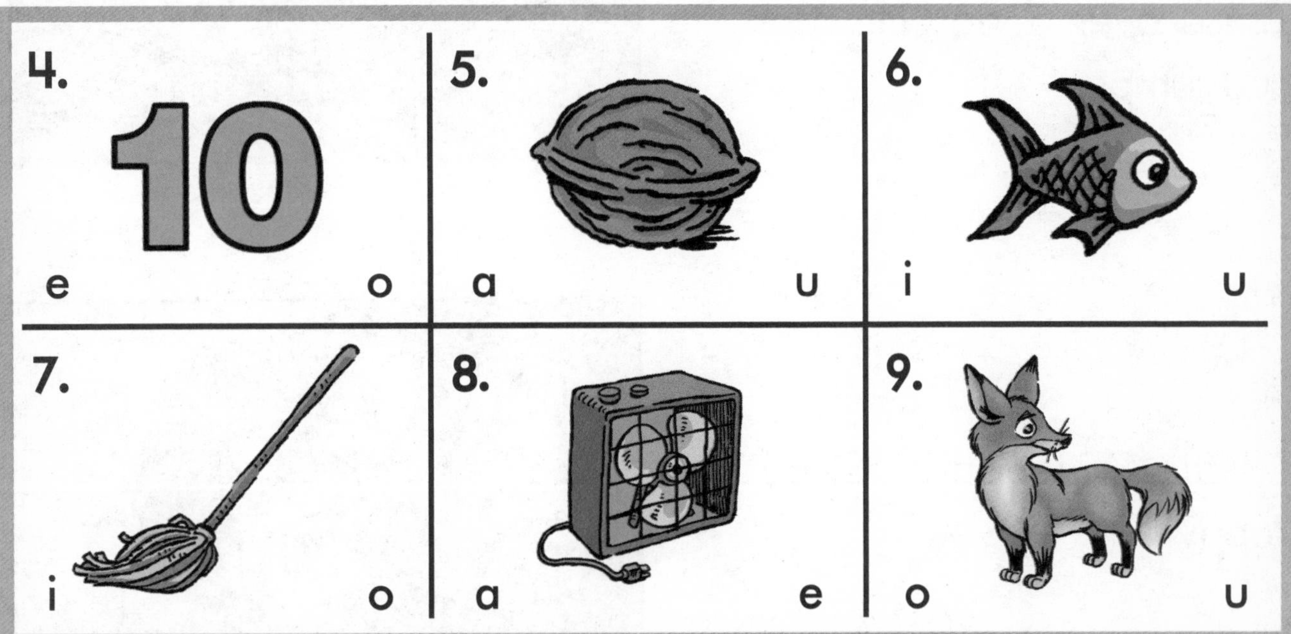


**10.**

Little Critter plays in the grass.
He sees something coming.
It cannot go fast.
What is it?

a squirrel
a turtle
a house

**11.**

The puppy plays in the grass.
A turtle comes near.
The puppy cannot see it.
Where is the turtle?

on a ball
in back of the puppy
under the snow

**Initial Consonants (1-3):** Have your child name each picture, listen to the beginning sound, and write the beginning letter below the picture.
**Short Vowels (4-9):** Have your child name each picture and listen to the vowel sound, then circle the correct vowel below the picture.
**Drawing Conclusions (10-11):** Have your child read the sentences in each box, then circle the phrase that makes the most sense.

# The Puppy Runs and Jumps

The puppy runs everywhere. He runs in the grass. He jumps over a log. He runs and jumps.

Little Critter says, "Stop, Puppy!"

The puppy runs and hides.

| 1. | 2. | 3. |
|---|---|---|
|  ____ | 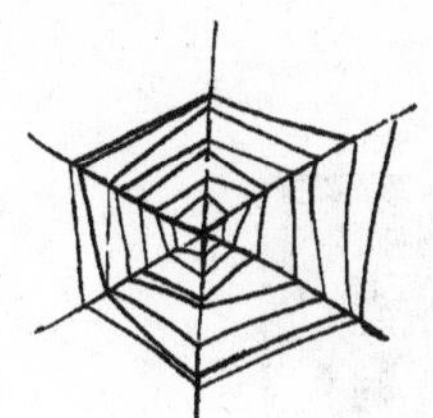 ____ |  ____ |

ran his three two

4. is ____________________
5. can ____________________
6. she ____________________
7. you ____________________

8.
The puppy is in the grass.
He wants to play.
The puppy will ________.

look at the grass
sleep in the sun
go find Little Critter

9.
Little Critter and the puppy see a ball.
They run to get it.
The puppy runs faster.
________ will get the ball.

Little Critter
The puppy

**Final Consonants (1-3):** Have your child name each picture, listen to the ending sound, and write the ending letter below the picture.
**Rhyming Words (4-7):** Have your child read the words at the top of the box, then read each numbered word. Ask your child to find the word at the top that rhymes with the numbered word, then write the rhyming word in the blank.
**Predicting Outcomes (8-9):** Have your child read the sentences in each box, then circle the phrase or word below that makes sense.

# Little Critter Looks Around

The puppy is hiding. Little Critter looks for the puppy.

He looks behind the house. He looks under the steps. He looks over the fence.

He looks in the doghouse.

He does not see the puppy. Where is the puppy?

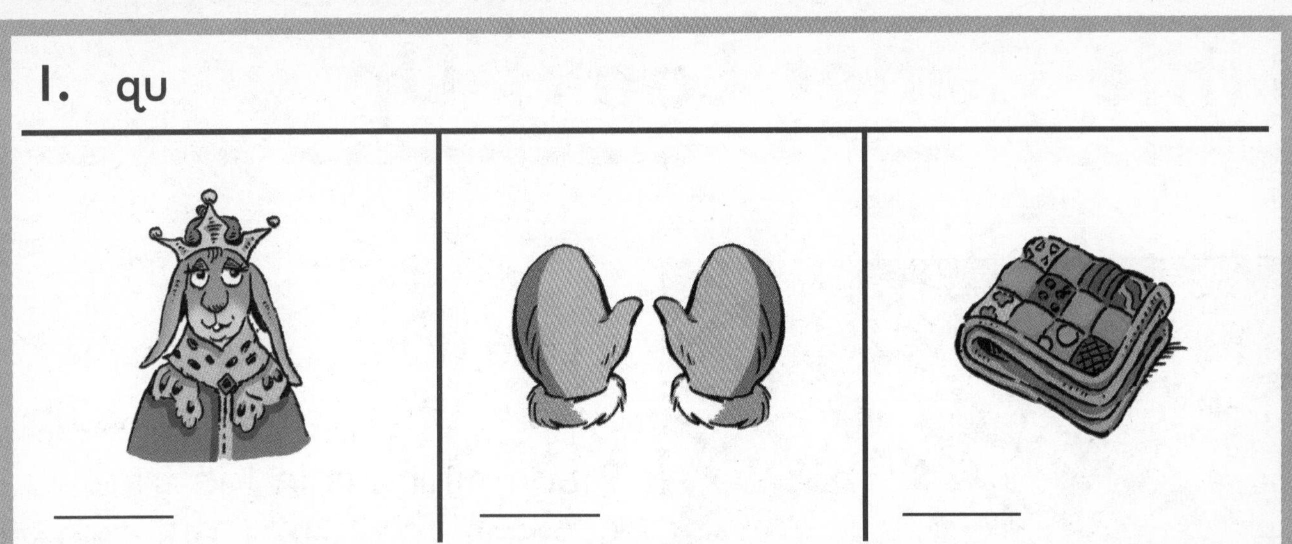


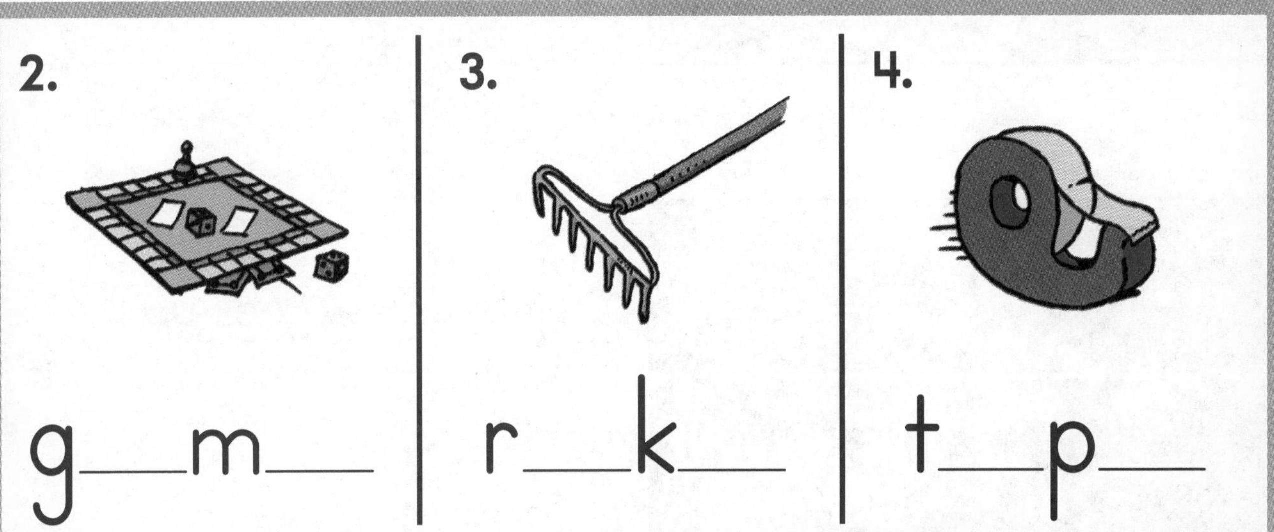


5. The ________ is hiding. house puppy

6. Little Critter looks behind the ________. house grass

7. Little Critter looks ________ the fence. over under

8. Little Critter does not ______ the puppy. run see

**Initial Consonants (1):** Review the sound of the letters **qu**. Have your child name each picture. Ask your child to write **qu** below each picture whose name begins with the **qu** sound. Have your child put an X directly on the picture that does not begin with the **qu** sound.
**Long Vowels (2-4):** Review the sound of long **a**. Have your child name each picture and listen to the vowel sound, then write the letters **a** and **e** to complete each picture name.
**Facts and Details (5-8):** Have your child read each sentence and, based on the story events, circle the correct answer.

# Little Critter Looks Up

Little Critter looks for the puppy. Little Critter looks up.

Something is in the tree. "What is it?" asks Little Critter. "I will go up."

Little Critter goes up the tree. A bird is in the tree! It is not his puppy.

Little Critter comes down.

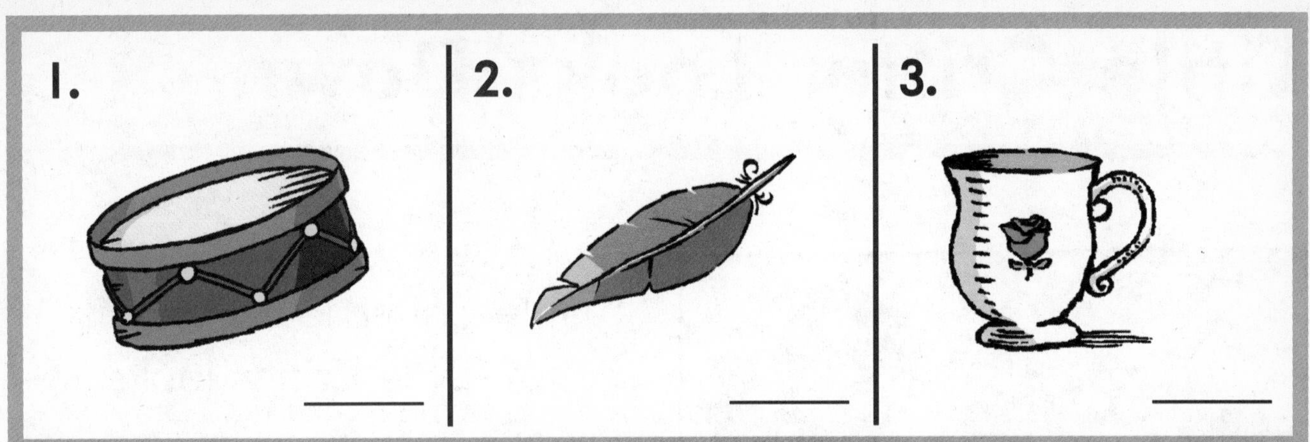

10. A ______________ is in the tree.
bird dog doll

11. He is my ______________.
mother house friend

**Final Consonants (1-3):** Have your child name each picture, listen to the ending sound, and write the ending letter beside the picture.
**Short Vowels (4-9):** Have your child name each picture and listen to the vowel sound, then circle the correct vowel below the picture.
**Context Clues (10-11):** Have your child read each sentence and circle the word that best completes the sentence, then write the word in the blank.

# Little Critter Looks Down

Little Critter looks for his puppy. Little Critter looks down.

Something is in there. "What is it?" asks Little Critter. "I will find out."

It is something big. Little Critter sees it look out at him. Little Critter jumps back.

It is not his puppy. It is a big dog. Little Critter runs fast.

1. fr

don't isn't can't

2. is not ________

3. do not ________

4. can not ________

5.
The water comes out.
It goes everywhere.
Little Critter runs away.
He ________ water.

likes doesn't like

6.
It is something that jumps.
It likes water.
It can't run fast.
It is a ________.

duck frog dog

**Blends (1):** Review the sound of the blend **fr**. Have your child name each picture, then write **fr** below each picture whose name begins with the **fr** sound. Have your child put an X directly on the picture that does not begin with the **fr** sound.
**Contractions (2-4):** Explain the concept of contractions to your child, then read the contractions at the top of the box. Have your child read each numbered pair of words, then write the contraction for the two words in the blank.
**Drawing Conclusions (5-6):** Have your child read the sentences in each box, then circle the word or phrase that makes the most sense.

# Little Critter Looks in the Town

Little Critter runs to the town. The town is called Critterville.

"I will look around here," says Little Critter.

Critterville has shops. Many critters work there.

"Is my puppy here somewhere?" asks Little Critter. "I will look."

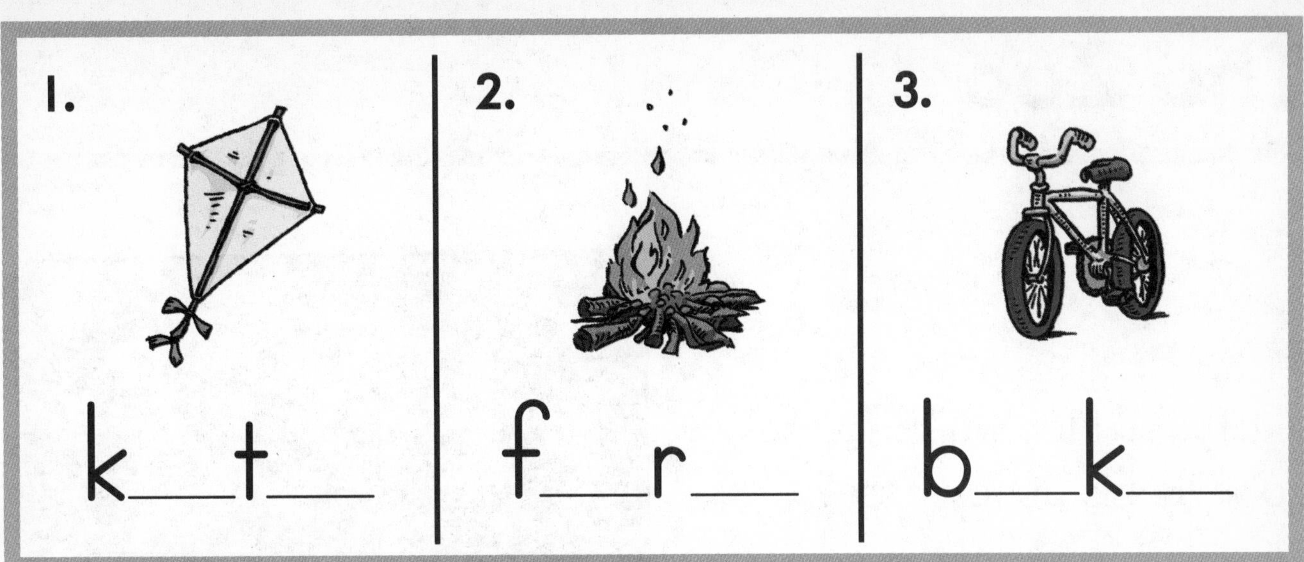

**Long Vowels (1-3):** Review the sound of long **i**. Have your child name each picture and listen to the vowel sound, then write the letters **i** and **e** to complete each picture name.
**Classification (4-6):** Have your child look at all four pictures or words in each row and circle the three that belong together.
**Picture Clues (7-8):** Ask your child to look at the picture and read the sentences in each box, then circle the sentence that your child would say to the puppy.

# The Zoo

Little Critter walks to the zoo. Is his puppy here?

He sees three yellow giraffes. He sees two orange tigers. He sees four gray elephants.

He does not see one little brown and white puppy.

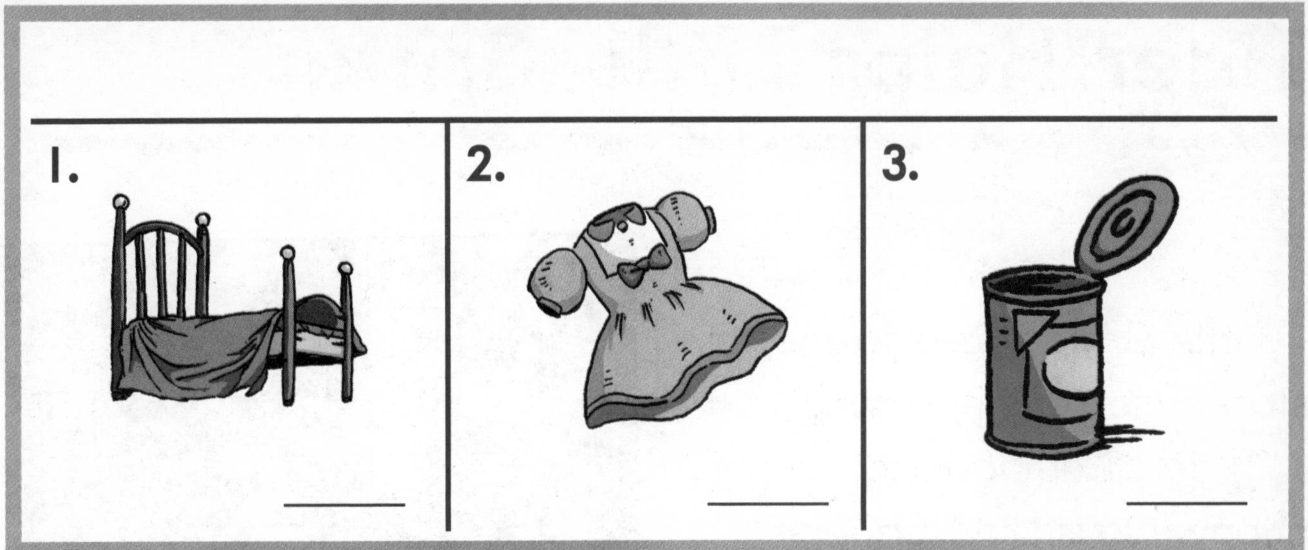


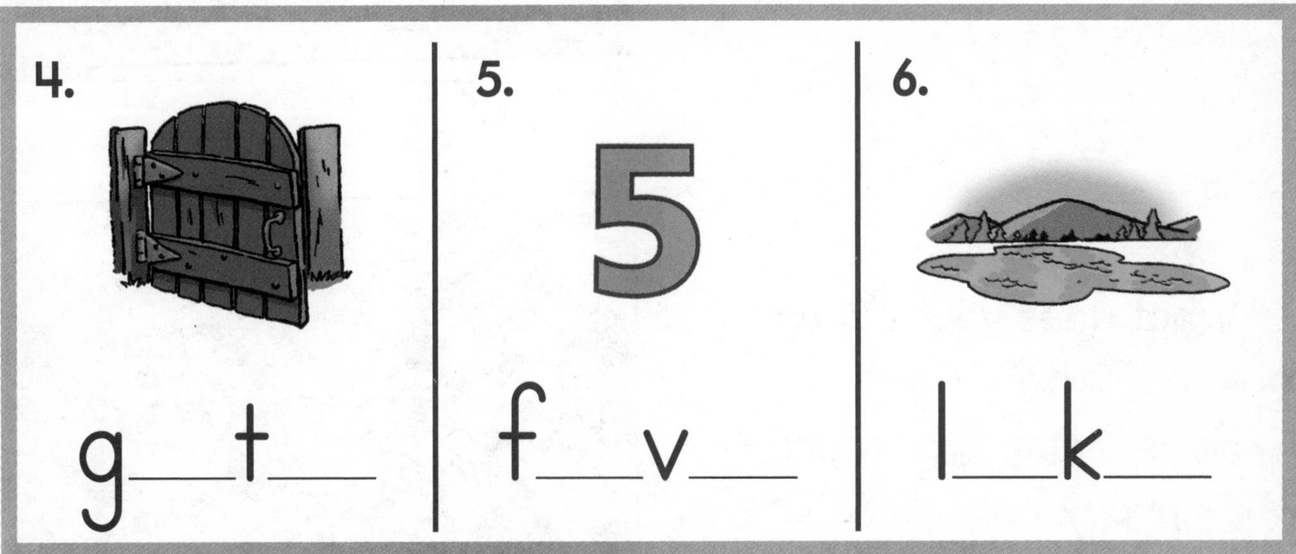


7.

Little Critter sees something run under the table.
He wants to see what it is.
What will Little Critter do?

play with a friend
get some hot water
look under the table

8.

The frog plays in the sun.
The frog is hot.
What will the frog do?

jump into cold water
jump up and down
sleep in the sun

**Final Consonants (1-3):** Have your child name each picture, listen to the ending sound, and write the ending letter below the picture.
**Long Vowels (4-6):** Have your child name each picture and listen to the vowel sound, then write the letters that complete the picture name.
**Predicting Outcomes (7-8):** Have your child read the sentences in each box, then circle the phrase below that makes sense.

# Tiger Helps Little Critter

Little Critter goes to the toy store. He sees his friend.

"Tiger, I am looking for my puppy," says Little Critter.

"What does your puppy look like?" asks Tiger.

"He is a little brown and white puppy," says Little Critter.

"He is not here," says Tiger. "I will help you look for him."

5. Tiger is in the ________. store zoo

6. Tiger asks ________ the puppy. about before

7. The puppy is ________. green brown

8. Tiger wants to ________. jump help

**Blends (1-3):** Have your child name each picture, listen to the beginning sound, and write the beginning blend below the picture.
**Consonant Digraphs (4):** Review the sound of the consonant digraph **wh**. Have your child name each picture, then write **wh** below each picture whose name begins with the **wh** sound. Have your child put an **X** directly on the picture that does not begin with the **wh** sound.
**Facts and Details (5-8):** Have your child read each sentence and, based on the story events, circle the correct answer.

# The Chase

Little Critter looks down the street. He sees something brown and white. "My puppy!" he says.

Little Critter and Tiger run. The puppy runs. The puppy jumps over a fence. Little Critter and Tiger jump over the fence.

The puppy runs to the pond. Little Critter and Tiger run to the pond, too.

They shout, "Puppy! Here, Puppy!"

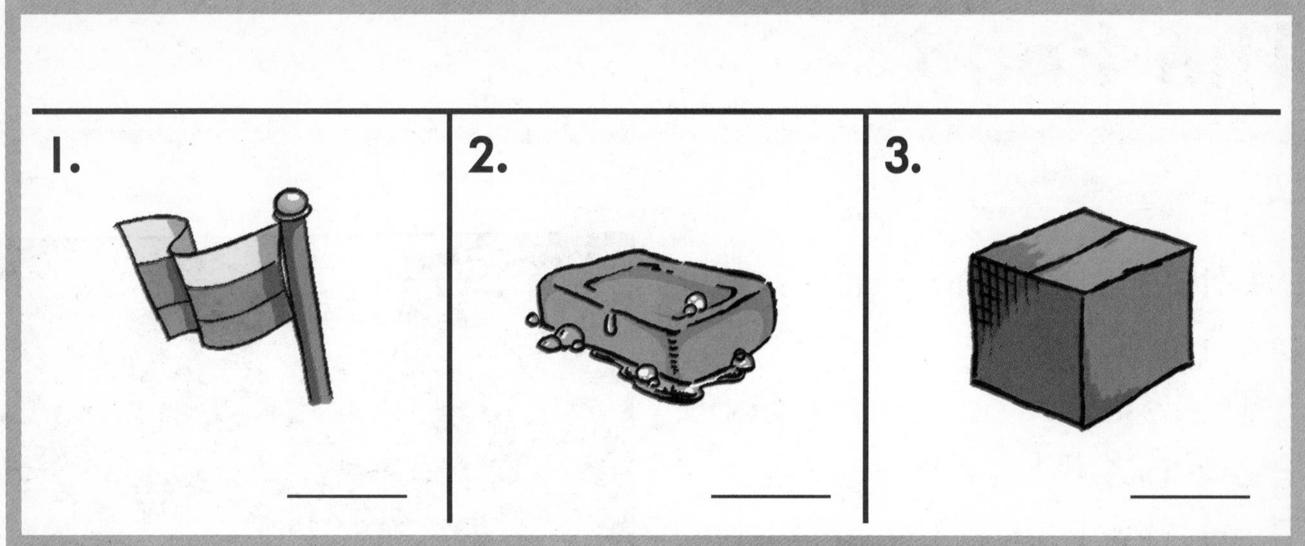


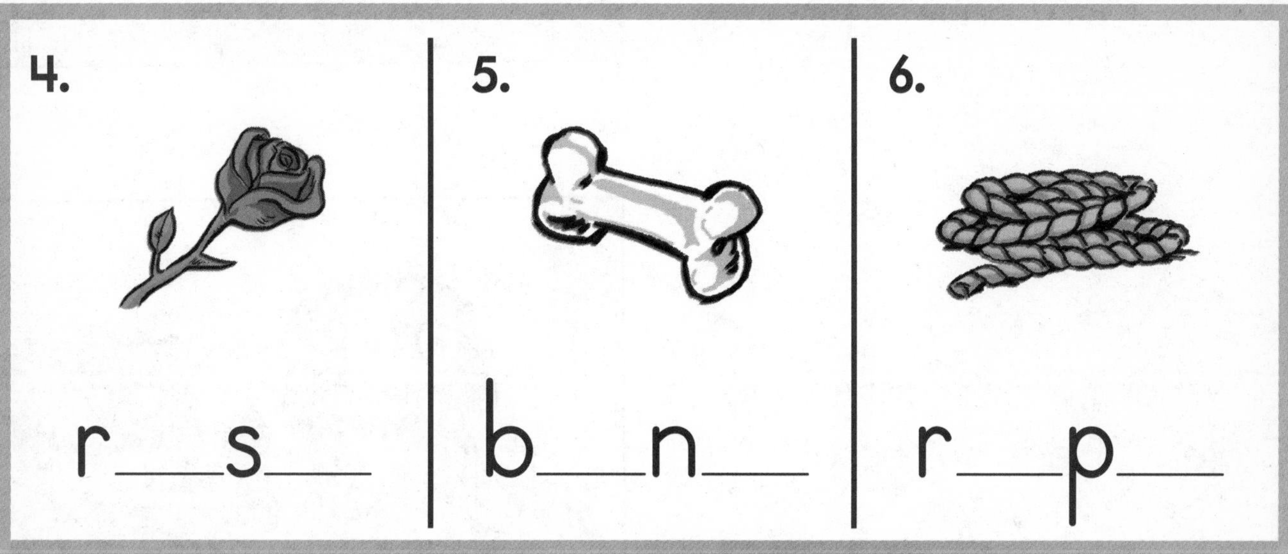


**7.**

The puppy is sleeping.
The sun is on his back.
He rolls over.
Where is the puppy?

on the grass
in a tree
in the water

**8.**

It has water in it.
Animals swim in it.
What is it?

a tree
a cup
a pond

**Final Consonants (1-3):** Have your child name each picture, listen to the ending sound, and write the ending letter below the picture.
**Long Vowels (4-6):** Review the sound of long **o**. Have your child name each picture and listen to the vowel sound, then write the letters **o** and **e** to complete each picture name.
**Drawing Conclusions (7-8):** Have your child read the sentences in each box, then circle the phrase that makes the most sense.

# The Pond

Little Critter and Tiger look around.

There are frogs at the pond. There are fish at the pond. There are butterflies at the pond. There is no puppy!

"Where is he?" asks Little Critter. "He is not here!"

"Maybe Gabby can help us," says Tiger.

1. th

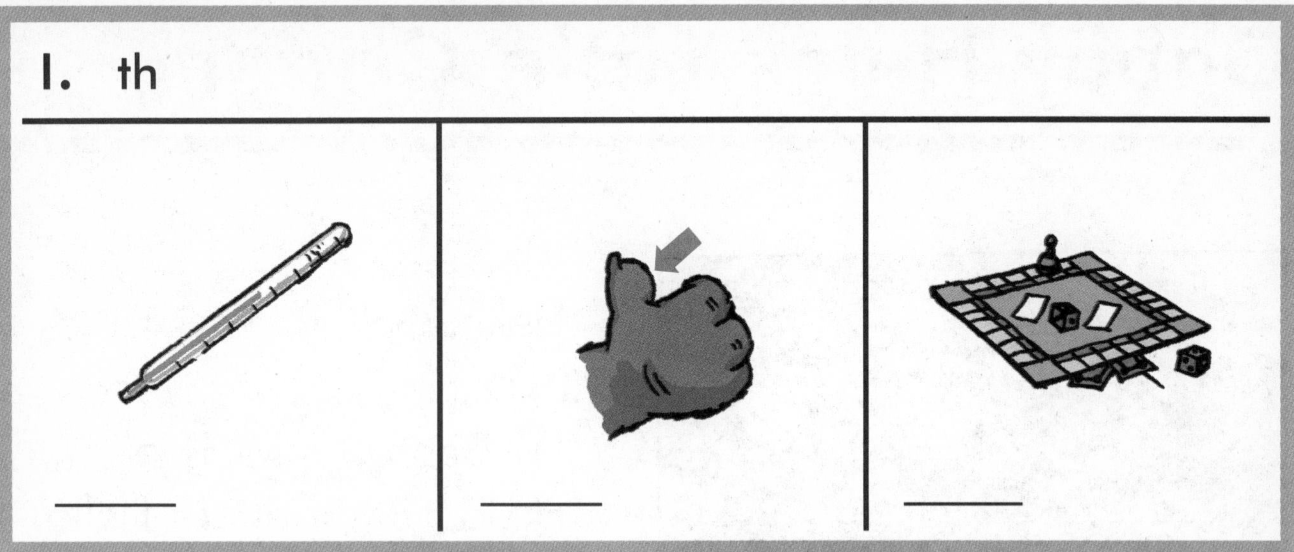

2.
Do you ________ to play?

want wants wanted

3.
Little Critter ________ with a ball.

play plays playing

4.
Little Critter is ________ for the puppy.

looks looked looking

5.
The frog has ________.

jumps jumped jumping

6.

**Consonant Digraphs (1):** Review the sound of the consonant digraph **th**. Have your child name each picture, then write **th** below each picture whose name begins with the **th** sound. Have your child put an **X** directly on the picture that does not begin with the **th** sound.
**Base Words and Endings (2-5):** Have your child read each sentence and circle the word that correctly completes the sentence.
**Sequence (6):** Have your child look at all three pictures, then write **1** below the event that would happen first, **2** below the event that would happen second, and **3** below the event that would happen third.

# Gabby Helps Little Critter

"Hello, Gabby," says Little Critter.

"Hi, Gabby," says Tiger.

"Hello, Little Critter. Hello, Tiger," says Gabby.

"My puppy is lost. Will you help us find him?" asks Little Critter.

"Yes, I will help," says Gabby. "Maybe the puppy is at our school."

1.

m__l__

2.

t__n__

3.

c__b__

| | | | | |
|---|---|---|---|---|
| 4. | **where** | tent | there | who |
| 5. | **hot** | not | her | new |
| 6. | **stop** | sun | play | pop |
| 7. | **some** | cold | come | said |
| 8. | **tent** | them | went | want |

9.

"Walk here, Puppy."
"Don't walk in here."

10.

"You can sleep here, Puppy."
"You can eat here."

**Long Vowels (1-3):** Review the sound of long **u**. Have your child name each picture and listen to the vowel sound, then write the letters **u** and **e** to complete each picture name.
**Rhyming Words (4-8):** Have your child read the words in each row, then circle the word that rhymes with the first word in each row.
**Picture Clues (9-10):** Ask your child to look at the picture and read sentences in each box, then circle the sentence that your child would say to the puppy.

# The School

The friends are at the school. They see Miss Kitty.

"Hello," says Little Critter. "We are looking for my puppy. Is he here at school?"

"I do not see a puppy here," says Miss Kitty.

They look under the desks. They look in the lunchroom. They look on the playground. They do not see the puppy.

1. ________________ go near the bee.
(Do not)

2. Her friend ________________ home .
(is not)

isn't
can't
don't

3.

looks
looked
looking

________________

4.

jumps
jumped
jumping

________________

5.

wants
wanted
wanting

________________

6. Miss Kitty is at the ________________.
house school pond

7. Little Critter says ________________ to Miss Kitty.
hello good-bye thank you

**Contractions (1-2):** Have your child read each sentence with the two words below the blank, then read the contractions in the box and write the correct one in each blank. Tell your child that one of the three contractions in the box will not be used.
**Base Words and Endings (3-5):** Have your child read the words in each box. Direct your child's attention to the circled word **look**, and explain the concept of base words. Have your child circle the base words in each box and then write the base word in the blank.
**Context Clues (6-7):** Have your child read each sentence and circle the word that best completes the sentence, then write the word in the blank.

# The Park

The friends go to the park. They see the puppy on the slide! Silly puppy!

They run to the puppy. The puppy runs away. Silly puppy!

The friends run around the park. They are tired. The puppy is not tired! He runs away again.

**Consonant Digraphs (1-3):** Have your child name each picture, listen to the beginning sound, and write the beginning consonant digraph in the blank below the picture.
**Long Vowels (4-6):** Have your child name each picture and listen to the vowel sound, then write the letters that complete the picture name.
**Picture Clues (7-8):** Ask your child to read the sentences in each box and circle the sentence that best describes the picture.

# Good-bye

"I have to go home now," says Gabby.

"I have to go home, too," says Tiger.

"Good-bye," says Little Critter. "Thank you for helping. I will keep looking."

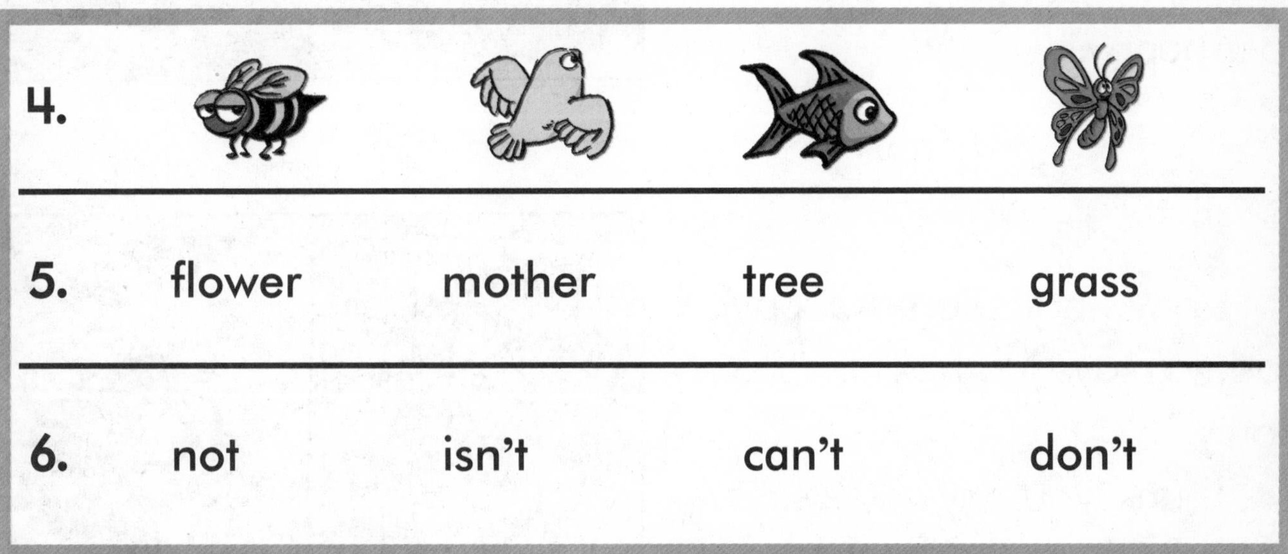

**Blends (1-3):** Have your child name each picture, listen to the beginning sound, and write the beginning blends below the picture.
**Classification (4-6):** Have your child look at all four pictures or words in each row and circle the three that belong together.
**Sequence (7):** Have your child look at all three pictures, then write **1** below the event that would happen first, **2** below the event that would happen second, and **3** below the event that would happen third.

# The Market

Little Critter walks past the market. Mr. Molini works there.

"Hello, Mr. Molini," says Little Critter. "I am looking for my lost puppy."

"I have not seen a puppy today," says Mr. Molini. "I am sorry."

"Thank you anyway," says Little Critter.

"Good-bye," says Mr. Molini.

"Good-bye," says Little Critter.

1. sh

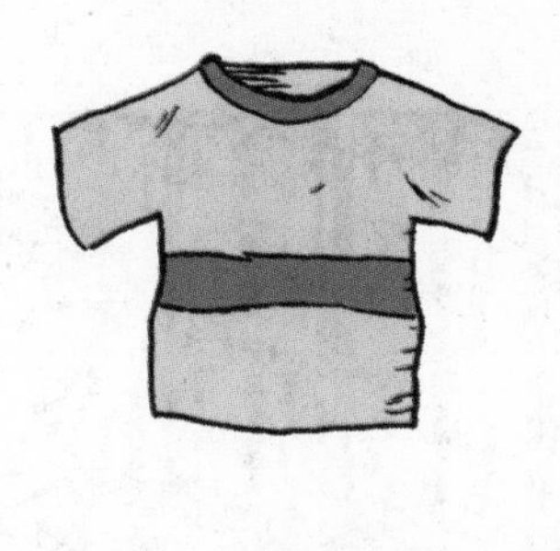

2.
Little Critter has ________ running.
stop stops stopped

3.
A squirrel ________ down the tree.
come comes coming

4.
The puppy is ________ very fast.
run runs running

5.
I don't ________ that bee.
like likes liked

6.
The puppy jumps and plays.
He runs fast.
He gets tired.
What will he do next?

run faster
play tag
go to sleep

7.
Little Critter and the puppy are playing.
A bee is coming. It is something they do not like.
What will they do next?

run away
play with the bee
run at the bee

**Consonant Digraphs (1):** Review the sound of the consonant digraph **sh**. Have your child name each picture, then write **sh** below each picture whose name begins with the **sh** sound. Have your child put an X directly on the picture that does not begin with the **sh** sound.
**Base Words and Endings (2-5):** Have your child read each sentence and circle the word that correctly completes the sentence.
**Predicting Outcomes (6-7):** Have your child read the sentences in each box, then circle the phrase below that makes sense.

# Walking Home

Little Critter walks home. He is tired. He is sad.

His puppy is not at the market or the pond. His puppy is not at the school or the zoo.

"My puppy ran away," says Little Critter.

1.

____

2.

____

3.

____

4. Where is Little Critter?

H____ is in his room.

5. Where is Little Sister?

Sh____ is not here.

6.

They are good to play with.

You cannot play with them.

7.

They are good to walk on.

Do not walk on them.

**Blends (1-3):** Have your child name each picture, listen to the beginning sound, and write the beginning blend in the blank below the picture.
**Long Vowels (4-5):** Review the sound of long **e**. Have your child read each item and decide what the incomplete word should be. Have your child write the letter **e** to complete the word.
**Picture Clues (6-7):** Direct your child to read the sentences in each box and circle the sentence that best describes the picture.

# A Happy Surprise

Little Critter goes into the house.

"Did you find your puppy?" asks his mom.

"I cannot find him. He is lost."

"I am sorry, Little Critter. Keep looking. You will find him," says his mom.

Little Critter looks out the window. "I see my puppy!" It is a happy surprise.

7. eating jumping walking running

8. three one happy two

9. to too three two

10. Here is a ________________ flower.
tired pretty fast

11. I ________________ tag with my friend.
rolled stopped played

**Short Vowels (1-6):** Have your child name each picture and listen to the vowel sound, then circle the correct vowel below the picture.
**Classification (7-9):** Have your child read all four words in each row and circle the three that belong together.
**Context Clues (10-11):** Have your child read each sentence and circle the word that best completes the sentence, then write the word in the blank.

# Dad's Flowers

The puppy is in the yard. He is digging in the flowers.

"Puppy! I am happy to see you!" says Little Critter. "But those are Dad's pretty flowers!"

The puppy looks at Little Critter. The puppy is very muddy. He does not look pretty.

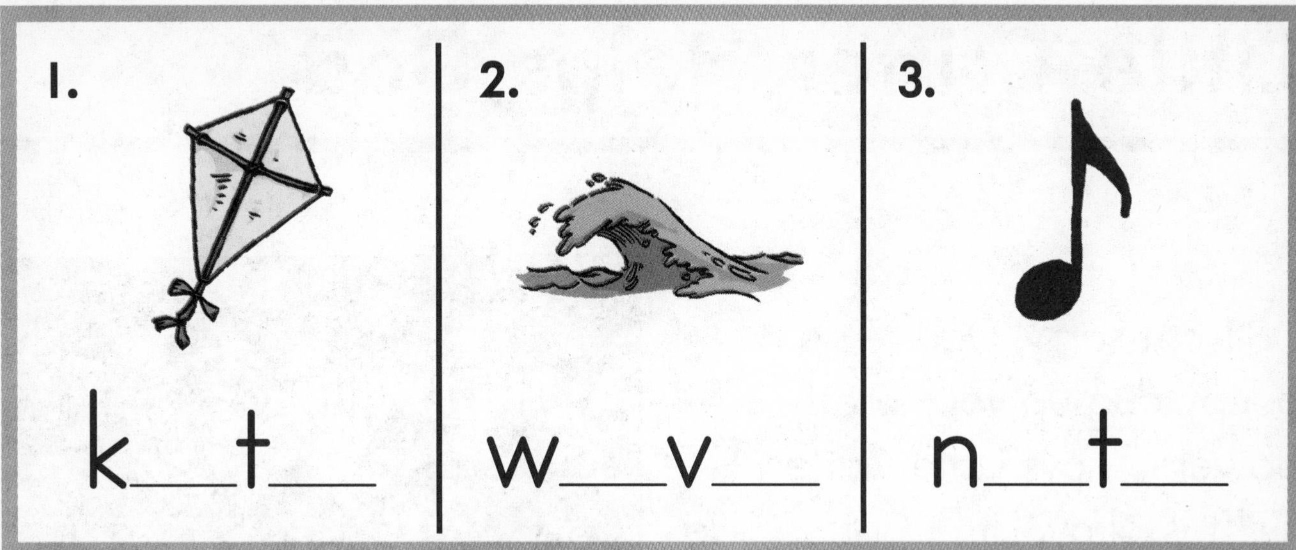


other bee try day

4. fly ______________ 5. play ______________

6. mother ______________ 7. tree ______________

8. The puppy is in the ________. yard house

9. Little Critter ________ the puppy. holds sees

10. The puppy digs ________ the flowers. up down

11. The puppy ________ muddy. is runs

**Long Vowels (1-3):** Have your child name each picture and listen to the vowel sound, then write the letters that complete the picture name.
**Rhyming Words (4-7):** Have your child read the words at the top of the box, then read each numbered word. Ask your child to find the word at the top that rhymes with the numbered word, then write the rhyming word in the blank.
**Facts and Details (8-11):** Have your child read each sentence and, based on the story events, circle the correct answer.

# Little Critter Helps Dad

“I am sorry, Dad. The puppy dug up your pretty flowers,” says Little Critter.

“It is okay, Little Critter. He is only a puppy,” says Dad.

Dad fixes the flowers. Little Critter helps. They work hard together.

“Thank you, Little Critter,” says Dad. “You are a good helper. Now I think your puppy needs some help to get clean.”

1. ch

2.

plays
played
playing

3.

walks
walked
walking

4.

rolls
rolled
rolling

5.

It is little.
It can fly.
It is not good to play with.
What is it?

a kite
a bee
a flower

6.

Gabby runs fast.
Tiger runs fast.
Little Critter runs to get them.
What are they doing?

playing tag
eating flowers
looking for birds

**Consonant Digraphs (1):** Review the sound of the consonant digraph **ch**. Have your child name each picture, then write **ch** below each picture whose name begins with the **ch** sound. Have your child put an X directly on the picture that does not begin with the **ch** sound.
**Base Words and Endings (2-4):** Have your child read the words in each box, circle the base words, and write the base word in the blank.
**Drawing Conclusions (5-6):** Have your child read the sentences in each box, then circle the phrase that makes the most sense.

# The Bath

It is time for the puppy to have a bath. Little Critter runs the water. He puts the puppy in the water.

The puppy does not like the water. The puppy does not like the soap. The puppy does not like the brush.

The puppy splashes and splashes. Water is everywhere.

Little Critter is wet. The puppy is clean!

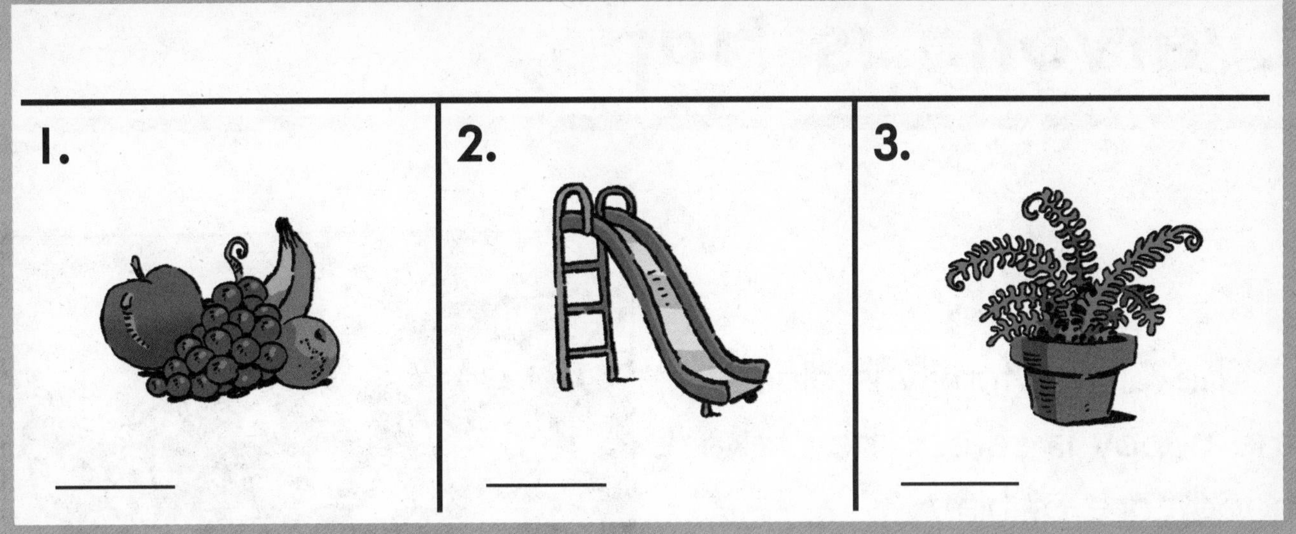


4. do not ____________ 5. was not ____________

6. is not ____________ 7. did not ____________

**Blends (1-3):** Have your child name each picture, listen to the beginning sound, and write the beginning blend below the picture.
**Contractions (4-7):** Have your child read the two words beside each blank, then write the contraction for the words in the blank.
**Sequence (8):** Have your child look at all three pictures, then write 1 below the event that would happen first, 2 below the event that would happen second, and 3 below the event that would happen third.

# Everyone is Happy

The Critter family is glad the puppy is safe. They take good care of him.

Mom pets the puppy. Dad gives him a big bone. Little Sister gives the puppy food.

Little Critter gives the puppy cold water.

"I will not let my puppy run away again," says Little Critter. "I will be more careful."

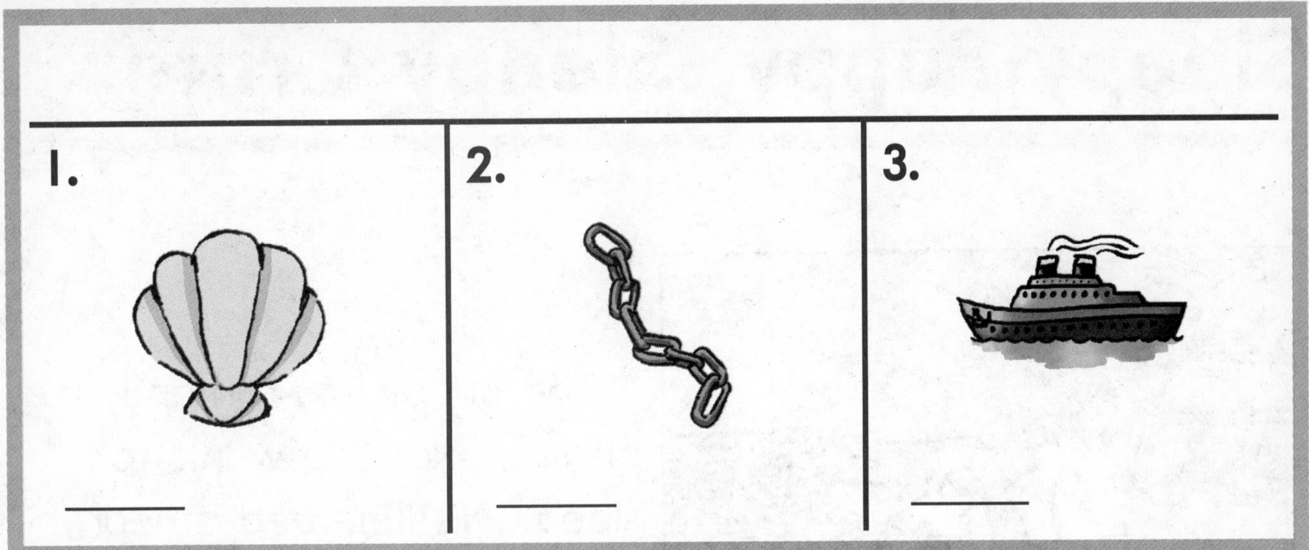

| | | |
|---|---|---|
| 7. Mom __________ the puppy. | pets | walks |
| 8. Dad gives him a __________ bone. | big | blue |
| 9. Little Sister __________ him food. | eats | gives |
| 10. Little Critter gives him __________. | water | toys |

**Consonant Digraphs (1-3):** Have your child name each picture, listen to the beginning sound, and write the beginning consonant digraph in the blank below the picture.
**Long Vowels (4-6):** Have your child name each picture and listen to the vowel sound, then write the letters that complete the picture name.
**Facts and Details (7-10):** Have your child read each sentence and, based on the story events, circle the correct answer.

# Sleepy Puppy, Sleepy Critter

The puppy has run and played. Now he wants to sleep. His little bed is near.

Puppy goes to the bed. It is a soft bed. It is a warm bed. Puppy likes to sleep in it. In he goes.

Puppy likes his bed. He likes to sleep there.

Little Critter likes to sleep there, too.

1. The mother bird ______________ in her nest.
was not

2. The sun ______________ come out all day.
did not

| 3. | flower | butterfly | frog | fish |
|---|---|---|---|---|
| 4. | game | doll | birds | kite |
| 5. | over | under | on | white |

6.
A little snow is on the grass.
The hot sun comes out.
What will the snow do?

go away
get very hard
stay cold and white

7.
Little Critter wants to give Little Sister something.
He wants it to be pretty.
What will Little Critter give Little Sister?

a bee
some water
a flower

**Contractions (1-2):** Have your child read each sentence with the two words below the blank, then write the contraction for the words in the blank.
**Classification (3-5):** Have your child read all four words in each row and circle the three that belong together.
**Predicting Outcomes (6-7):** Have your child read the sentences in each box, then circle the phrase below that makes sense.

# Sounds You Know

**Initial and Final Consonants, Blends, and Digraphs (1-10):** Have your child name each picture and listen to the beginning and ending sounds. Ask your child to write the letters that stand for the beginning and ending sounds of each picture name in the appropriate blanks.

# Words You Know

| 1. | 2. | 3. |
|---|---|---|
| run<br>sun<br>fun | friend<br>faster<br>flower | big<br>birds<br>ball |
| **4.** | **5.** | **6.** |
| dog<br>did<br>don't | pond<br>play<br>day | puppy<br>cup<br>sun |
| **7.** | **8.** | **9.** |
| to<br>too<br>two | fish<br>frog<br>butterfly | go<br>game<br>give |
| **10.** | **11.** | **12.** |
| hot<br>not<br>now | goes<br>grass<br>good | three<br>there<br>them |
| **13.** | **14.** | **15.** |
| yellow<br>yard<br>yes | be<br>big<br>bee | could<br>come<br>cold |

**Word Recognition (1-15):** Have your child name each picture and circle the word that names or best describes the picture.

# Where Are You From?

"Good-bye, Mom!" called Little Critter.

"Good-bye, Little Critter. Have a nice day," said Mom.

Little Critter opened the door.

"Meow!"

Little Critter jumped back. There was a cat sitting on the doormat. She had black and orange spots.

"Hello, Cat. Where are you from?" asked Little Critter. "I would like to play, but I have to go to school!"

Little Critter patted the cat on the head. Then he started walking to school.

## Reading and Thinking

1. This story is about

   ____ school

   ____ a cat

   ____ a dog

2. The cat has

   ____ a mouse

   ____ stripes

   ____ spots

## Working with Words

| 1. | 2. | 3. |
|---|---|---|
| play<br>day  | cat<br>hat  | can<br>ran  |

4. She h___d black and orange spots.

5. Little Critter j___mped back.

**Reading and Thinking** Main Idea (1): Have your child complete the sentence by writing a check beside the correct answer. Picture Clues (2): Have your child look at the picture and complete the sentence by writing a check beside the correct answer.
**Working with Words** Initial Consonants (1-3): Have your child name each picture and circle the word that names it. Short Vowels (4-5): Have your child read each sentence, then complete each unfinished word by writing the missing vowel.

# The Shadow

The cat followed Little Critter. He did not see her. She sneaked up behind him.

"Oh, no!" said Little Critter. His feet got tangled. He tripped and fell over the cat.

She licked Little Critter's face. She purred. She meowed.

"You are a very pretty cat," said Little Critter. "You should go home. Your family will miss you."

The cat followed Little Critter all the way to school.

## Reading and Thinking

1. Little Critter did not see the _____.

   ____ hat

   ____ cat

   ____ home

2. Where is Little Critter going?

   ____ out to play

   ____ on a bus

   ____ to school

## Working with Words

1\.

c___t

2\.

___p

3\.

L___ttle
Cr___tter

not race kiss meet

4. feet ____________________
5. got ____________________
6. face ____________________
7. miss ____________________

**Reading and Thinking** Drawing Conclusions (1): Have your child complete the sentence by writing a check beside the correct answer. Predicting Outcomes (2): Have your child read the question and, based on the story events, write a check beside the correct answer.
**Working with Words** Short Vowels (1-3): Have your child name each picture, listen to the vowel sound, and write the vowel that completes the picture name. Rhyming Words (4-7): Have your child read the words at the top of the exercise, then read each numbered word. Ask your child to find the word at the top that rhymes with the numbered word, then write the rhyming word in the blank.

# A Visitor

Little Critter told the cat she could not come to school. She followed him anyway.

"Little Critter, you brought a friend to school," said Miss Kitty.

"I don't know who this cat belongs to," said Little Critter.

The little cat jumped from desk to desk. She wanted to meet everyone.

She jumped on Miss Kitty's desk. She rubbed against Miss Kitty and purred.

"This is a lovely cat," said Miss Kitty. "She can visit just for today."

## Reading and Thinking

1. Why was the cat at school?

   ____ Miss Kitty brought it.

   ____ She followed Little Critter.

   ____ The cat was hungry.

2. What did the cat do to Miss Kitty?

   ________________________________

   ________________________________

## Working with Words

1. The ________ is Little Critter's friend.
   cat   bat

2. Let's read a good ________.
   book   look

---

| | | | |
|---|---|---|---|
| 3. just | don't | school | must |
| 4. him | Jim | boy | they |
| 5. could | bed | desk | would |

**Reading and Thinking** Cause and Effect (1): Have your child read the question and write a check beside the correct answer. Facts and Details (2): Have your child read the question and write the answer in the blanks.
**Working with Words** Initial Consonants (1-2): Have your child read each sentence and write the word that best completes it. Rhyming Words (3-5): Have your child read the words in each row. Ask your child to circle the word that rhymes with the first word in each row.

# The Class Project

"How can we find the owner of this cat?" Miss Kitty asked.

Molly answered, "We could make signs."

"And hang them up around Critterville," said Maurice.

"Good idea! This will be a class project," said Miss Kitty.

Little Critter was having trouble working. The cat was lying on his paper.

Miss Kitty found a box and put her sweater in it. The cat curled up inside the box for a nap.

## Reading and Thinking

1. This story is about
   ____ how Miss Kitty teaches Math.
   ____ how the class will find the cat's owner.
   ____ Little Critter's desk at school.

2. What did the class do to help the cat?
   ____ They made signs.
   ____ They fed her.
   ____ They put her outside.

## Working with Words

| 1. | 2. | 3. |
|---|---|---|
| bus<br>but | can<br>cat | had<br>hat |

don't    can't    let's    didn't

4. can not ____________
5. do not ____________
6. did not ____________
7. let us ____________

**Reading and Thinking** Main Idea (1): Have your child complete the sentence by writing a check beside the correct answer. Drawing Conclusions (2): Have your child read the question and write a check beside the correct answer.
**Working with Words** Final Consonants (1-3): Have your child name each picture and circle the word that names it. Contractions (4-7): Have your child read the contractions at the top of the exercise, then read each numbered pair of words. Have your child write the contraction for the two words in the blank.

# Hanging Signs

That afternoon, Miss Kitty and the class walked through Critterville.

They put a sign in the window of Mr. Hogley's Hardware Store. They put a sign on the door at Stork's Toy Shop.

Little Critter tried to put a sign up at Mr. Rubble's Junkyard. Puddles, the big junkyard dog, barked a little too loud.

"I'll find another spot for my sign," said Little Critter.

## Reading and Thinking

1. Where did the class put signs?

______________________________

______________________________

2. Why did Little Critter want to find another spot for his sign?

___ He was afraid of Puddles.

___ Mr. Rubble was mean.

___ He didn't see a door.

## Working with Words

| 1. | 2. | 3. |
|---|---|---|
|   |  | 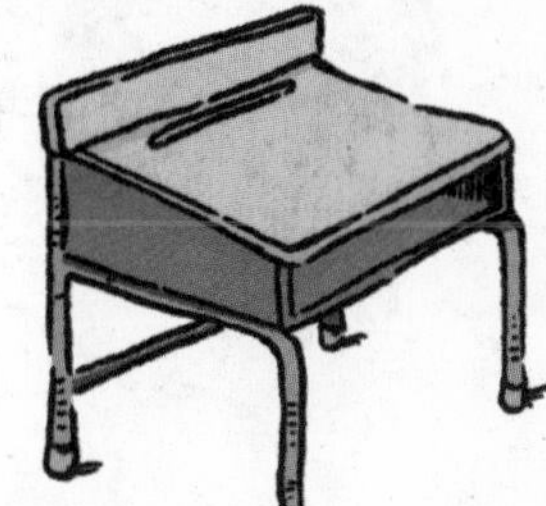 |
| sh___p | M___lly | d___sk |

4. asked
   asking

   ______________

5. walks
   walked

   ______________

6. barks
   barking

   ______________

**Reading and Thinking** Facts and Details (1): Have your child read the question and write the answer in the blank. Drawing Conclusions (2): Have your child read the question and write a check beside the correct answer.
**Working with Words** Short Vowels (1-3): Have your child name each picture, listen to the vowel sound, and write the vowel that completes the picture name. Base Words and Endings (4-6): Have your child read the words, circle the base words, and write each base word in the blank.

# A Lot of Cats

That night, Little Critter told Mom, Dad, and Little Sister about the cat.

"She's in the clubhouse," said Little Critter. "She won't be any trouble."

They looked in the clubhouse. There was not just one cat. There were eight!

"Meow! Meow!"

"Little Critter, your stray cat is now a mother cat," said Mr. Critter.

"Can we keep the kittens?" asked Little Sister.

"Eight cats is a lot of cats," said Mrs. Critter. "We must find homes for them."

# Reading and Thinking

1.

[1] ____ Little Sister asked to keep the kittens.

[2] ____ There were eight cats in the clubhouse.

[3] ____ They looked in the clubhouse.

2. The ________________ cat had kittens.

mother must

3. There were ________________ cats.

egg eight

# Working with Words

1. ___other

2. ___ittens

3. ___ouse

4. glass grass

5. desk drink

6. sleep stop

**Reading and Thinking** Sequence (1): Have your child read the sentences and number them to show the order of events in the story. Context Clues (2-3): Have your child read each sentence and write the word that best completes it.
**Working with Words** Initial Consonants (1-3): Have your child name each picture, listen to the beginning sound, and write the letter that completes the picture name. Blends (4-6): Have your child name each picture and circle the word that names or best describes it.

# A New Friend

The next morning, Little Critter was going to take his puppy for a walk. As soon as Little Critter put the leash on him, the puppy ran out the door.

The puppy's ears perked up. He pulled Little Critter to the clubhouse.

Little Critter did not want the puppy to frighten the kittens.

When the puppy saw the colorful kittens, he stopped. He sniffed them gently. The puppy was a friend.

"Good dog!" said Little Critter.

# Reading and Thinking

1. We took the puppy for a ________________.

   wall walk

2. The boy ________________ the ball to his friend.

   their threw

3. Don't ________________ that string away.

   those throw

# Working with Words

1. three
   throw

   3

2. flew
   flower

3. at
   eat

# Learning to Study

1. ecd ________________
2. hgf ________________
3. pon ________________
4. srt ________________

**Reading and Thinking** Context Clues (1-3): Have your child read each sentence and write the word that best completes it.
**Working with Words** Vowel Digraphs and Dipthongs (1-3): Have your child name each picture and circle the word that names or best describes it. **Learning to Study** Alphabetical Order (1-4): Have your child write each set of letters in alphabetical order.

# A Mouse Problem

One day, Little Critter and his mom were at Molini's Market. Suddenly, a mouse ran in front of Mrs. Critter.

"A mouse!" she screamed.

Mr. Molini said, "I am sorry! I have a mouse problem."

Mrs. Critter said, "I think I know how to solve this problem. Our kittens are growing. Soon, they will be ready to leave their mother. Then they can go to new homes."

"I need a cat to chase the mice," said Mr. Molini.

Mr. Molini went to the Critters' house. He chose Stripe, a little gray kitten with tiger stripes.

## Reading and Thinking

I. This story takes place at

___ school. ___ the market. ___ the farm.

2. Why did Mr. Molini need a cat?

___ He needed someone to walk with.

___ He needed someone to watch the store.

___ He wanted a cat to chase mice.

## Working with Words

| I. | 2. | 3. |
|---|---|---|
|  |  |  |
| r___s___ | b___t___ | m___l___ |

I. Do you know ______________ she lives?

there where

2. Is ______________ your cat over there?

that what

**Reading and Thinking** Drawing Conclusions (1): Have your child complete the sentence by writing a check beside the correct answer. Cause and Effect (2): Have your child read the question and write a check beside the correct answer.
**Working with Words** Long Vowels (1-3): Have your child name each picture, listen to the vowel sound, and write the letters that complete the picture name. Consonant Digraphs (4-5): Have your child read each sentence and write the word that best completes it.

# Chocolate Footprints

Mrs. Critter was in the kitchen. She was making a chocolate cake and humming a tune.

Little Critter walked into the kitchen. The six kittens followed him.

"Mom, can I help make the cake?" asked Little Critter.

"Yes, Little Critter, you can help," answered his mom. "You can mix the batter."

Little Critter tried to mix the batter, but he spilled some by mistake. The kittens liked the batter. They stepped in it and made batter footprints everywhere!

"Maybe you should take the kittens outside to play," said Mrs. Critter.

## Reading and Thinking

1. This story is about

   ____ feeding the kittens.

   ____ cleaning the house.

   ____ baking a cake.

2. Little Critter wanted to

   ____ run. ____ play. ____ help.

## Working with Words

1. Can your pet do a ____ick?

2. Who ____osed the window?

3. A farm is a ____ace for animals.

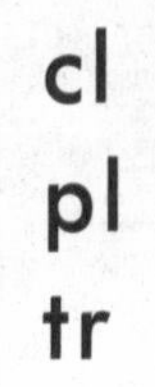

---

4. The boy's cat ______________ on his bed.

   sleeps sleeping

5. I ______________ at the funny picture.

   looks looked

6. He is ______________ the children a book.

   showed showing

**Reading and Thinking** Main Idea (1): Have your child complete the sentence by writing a check beside the correct answer. Drawing Conclusions (2): Have your child complete the sentence by writing a check beside the correct answer.
**Working with Words** Blends(1-3): Have your child read each sentence and look at the blends in the small box, then complete each unfinished word by writing the missing blend. Base Words and Endings (4-6): Have your child read each sentence and write the word that correctly completes it.

# A Home for Two

Outside, Mr. Critter was planting a tree. Little Critter wanted to help. The kittens climbed all over the new tree. They climbed on Little Critter and Mr. Critter, too.

"These kittens sure like to play," said Mr. Critter.

The twins, Maurice and Molly, ran into the yard.

"Hello!" they said. "We have good news. Our parents said that we can each adopt a kitten!"

"That is good news!" said Mr. Critter, as he pulled a kitten off his leg.

Maurice and Molly chose two spotted kittens that looked like the mother cat. They named the kittens Speckle and Freckle.

# Reading and Thinking

1. What was Mr. Critter doing in the yard?

    ____ He was planting flowers.

    ____ He was planting a tree.

    ____ He was cutting the grass.

2. When I ________________ my eyes, I can't see.

    could    cover

3. The funny kittens ________________ the tree.

    climb    chose

# Working with Words

1. My bed h___s three covers on it.

2. He g___t a balloon at the circus.

---

ball    balls    top    tops

3.  ____________

4.  ____________

5.  ____________

6. 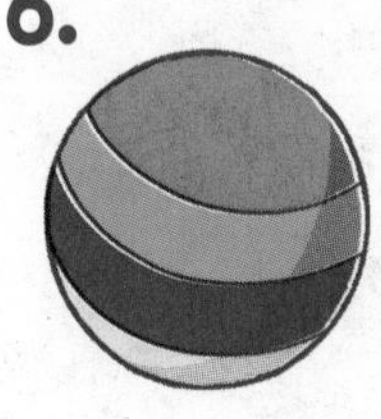 ____________

**Reading and Thinking** Drawing Conclusions (1): Have your child read the question and write a check beside the correct answer. Context Clues (2-3): Have your child read each sentence and write the word that best completes it.
**Working with Words** Short Vowels (1-2): Have your child read each sentence, then complete each unfinished word by writing the missing vowel. Singular and Plural (3-6): Have your child read the words at the top of the exercise. Ask your child to look at each picture and, in the blank, write the word that names it.

# The Bully

At school, Malcolm, the bully, came up to Little Critter.

"Meet me at your clubhouse after school," said Malcolm in a loud voice.

"Okay," said Little Critter. He was a little scared.

They met at the clubhouse. Malcolm picked up a kitten. He held it carefully and stroked its head.

"I didn't know that you liked animals!" said Little Critter.

"I would like to have a cat," said Malcolm, "but cats make my mother sneeze."

"Malcolm, you can come over any time to visit our cats," said Little Critter.

# Reading and Thinking

1. ____ Malcolm wanted to meet Little Critter.
   ____ Little Critter told Malcolm to come any time.
   ____ Malcolm petted a kitten.

2. Why can't Malcolm have a cat?
   ____ They make his mother sneeze.
   ____ Cats sneeze a lot.
   ____ He doesn't like cats.

# Working with Words

1. Grandma told ______________ a story.
   up us

2. We gave ______________ some flowers.
   then them

---

| | | | | |
|---|---|---|---|---|
| 3. | **met** | much | desk | pet |
| 4. | **pick** | why | sick | Molly |
| 5. | **came** | rose | name | come |
| 6. | **walk** | little | way | talk |

**Reading and Thinking** Sequence (1): Have your child read the sentences and number them to show the order of events in the story. Facts and Details (2): Have your child read the question and write a check beside the correct answer.
**Working with Words** Final Consonants (1-2): Have your child read each sentence and write the word that best completes it. Rhyming Words (3-6): Have your child read the words in each row, then circle the word that rhymes with the first word in each row.

# A Home at the Zoo?

The kittens were growing. Little Critter wanted to find good homes for the kittens. He thought the Critterville Zoo would be a fun place for them to live. He put the four kittens in a box and pulled them in his wagon.

"Can I help you?" asked Ms. Dingo, the zookeeper.

Little Critter said, "I have four kittens that need a good home."

The kittens peeked out of the box.

"Roooooaaaarrrrr!" A tiger let out a very mean growl. The kittens ducked back into the box.

"I'm afraid the zoo is not a good home for kittens," said Ms. Dingo.

## Reading and Thinking

1. Who did Little Critter talk to at the zoo?

______________________________________

2. What animal did Little Critter see at the zoo?

____ a kitten

____ a tiger

____ a lion

## Working with Words

1. _____en she saw the surprise, she laughed.
2. _____e threw the ball to me.
3. _____ank you for helping us.
4. _____is has been a good day.

| Sh |
|---|
| Th |
| Wh |

---

5. When I called the cat, it c____m____.
6. He m____d____ a new friend at school.
7. H____ can't find his new hat.
8. Do you l____k____ to eat apples?

**Reading and Thinking** Facts and Details (1): Have your child read the question and write the answer in the blank. Drawing Conclusions (2): Have your child read the question and write a check beside the correct answer.
**Working with Words** Consonant Digraphs (1-4): Have your child read each sentence and look at the consonant digraphs in the small box. Have your child complete each unfinished word by writing the missing consonant digraph. One of the consonant digraphs will be used twice.
Long Vowels (5-8): Have your child read each sentence, then complete each unfinished word by writing the missing letters.

# Stork's Toy Shop

Little Critter walked down the street to Stork's Toy Shop. There were all sorts of neat toys there. Mr. Stork, the owner, was very nice.

"Hello, Mr. Stork," said Little Critter.

"Hello, Little Critter," said Mr. Stork. "Would you like to buy a toy or a game today?"

"No, thank you," said Little Critter. "See, I have some kittens."

One of the kittens jumped out of the box. The kitten ran around the store and knocked down a display of bouncy balls. The balls bounced everywhere!

"Oops! This is not a good place for kittens," said Little Critter.

## Reading and Thinking

1. Which is not a good place for cats?

    ____ at home ____ in the yard ____ Stork's Toy Shop

2. I ______________ you will like the surprise.

    happy hope

3. There is glass in the ______________.

    without window

## Working with Words

| 1. | 2. | 3. |
|---|---|---|
| three<br>tree  | flowers<br>found  | sleep<br>stop  |

4. I have two ______________ for pets.
5. The brown ______________ likes to play.
6. One time it got stuck in a ______________.
7. The other cat does not like ______________.

| cat |
|---|
| cats |
| tree |
| trees |

**Reading and Thinking** Picture Clues (1): Have your child look at the picture that accompanies the story, then complete the unfinished sentence by writing a check beside the correct answer. Context Clues (2-3): Have your child read each sentence and write the word that best completes it. **Working with Words** Blends (1-3): Have your child name each picture and circle the word that names or best describes it. Singular and Plural (4-7): Have your child read the sentences and the words in the small box, then choose the word that makes sense in each sentence and write it in the blank.

# The Auto Repair Shop

Little Critter went to visit his dad's friend, Rusty. Rusty worked at the Critterville Auto Repair Shop.

"Hi, Little Critter," said Rusty. "What have you got there?"

"I have four kittens that need good homes," said Little Critter.

Rusty picked up a little orange kitten. "My, she sure is cute," said Rusty. "But the auto repair shop is not a safe place for kittens. Cars come in and out all the time. There are many sharp tools around here, too."

"You are right, Rusty," said Little Critter. "See you later."

## Reading and Thinking

1. Why didn't Rusty keep a kitten?

   ____ He is afraid of cats.

   ____ Cats make him sneeze.

   ____ His repair shop was not safe for kittens.

2. This story is about

   ____ the Auto Repair Shop. ____ the zoo.

   ____ the wagon.

## Working with Words

| 1. | 2. | 3. |
|---|---|---|
| think<br>trick  | fly<br>from  | sleep<br>stuck  |

4. We saw a good ________________ about a dog.

   know show

5. Are these your ________________?

   things time

6. ________________ is the man's house?

   Where Wish

**Reading and Thinking** Cause and Effect (1): Have your child read the question and write a check beside the correct answer. Main Idea (2): Have your child complete the sentence by writing a check beside the correct answer.
**Working with Words** Blends (1-3): Have your child name each picture and circle the word that names or best describes it. Consonant Digraphs (4-6): Have your child read each sentence and write the word that best completes it.

# The Karate Cat

Little Critter went to see his friend, Tiger, at the karate school. Tiger was really good at karate. He was a blackbelt.

"Hello, Little Critter," said Tiger. "What is in the box?"

"Hello," said Little Critter. "I have four kittens that need homes." Little Critter took one kitten out of the box. He placed it on the mat.

The kitten was frightened. She didn't know which way to run.

"My kitten looks scared. Maybe I better take her home!" said Little Critter.

## Reading and Thinking

1. Who was at the karate school? ______________________

______________________________________________

2. Little Critter has

___ one kitten. ___ two kittens. ___ four kittens.

## Working with Words

1. A place for animals to stay is a ____________.

pen pet

2. We asked ____________ how to get to the farm.

him his

3. We can hold the boxes in ____________ arms.

our out

---

pen pens pig pigs

4. ________ 5. ________ 6. ________ 7. ________

**Reading and Thinking** Drawing Conclusions (1): Have your child read the question and write the answer in the blank. Facts and Details (2): Have your child complete the sentence by writing a check beside the correct answer.
**Working with Words** Final Consonants (1-3): Have your child read each sentence and write the word that best completes it. Singular and Plural (4-7): Have your child read the words at the top of the exercise. Ask your child to look at each picture and write the word that names it in the blank.

# Mrs. Jones

Little Critter walked past Mr. Hogley's Hardware Store. A lady was reading one of the signs Little Critter's class put in the window. She said, "Found–female cat. Brown and orange spots. Call the Critter family at 555-1111."

"That sounds like my Patches!" said the lady. "She ran off last week."

"Hi, my name is Little Critter. Is your cat lost?"

"Yes, she is. My name is Mrs. Jones.
I think this might be my cat, Patches."

Mrs. Jones called Mrs. Critter to ask if she could come and see the cat that afternoon.

## Knowing the Words

| | | | | |
|---|---|---|---|---|
| 1. | see | look | watch | hear |
| 2. | yellow | orange | paint | black |
| 3. | cow | farm | sheep | pig |

## Reading and Thinking

1. Patches is Mrs. Jones'

   ____ cat.

   ____ little boy.

   ____ uncle.

2. Where will Mrs. Jones go this afternoon?

   ____ home.

   ____ to Little Critter's house.

   ____ to the store.

## Learning to Study

1. edf ____________________
3. lnm ____________________
2. jhi ____________________
4. zxy ____________________

**Knowing the Words** Classification (1-3): Have your child read all four words in each row and circle the three that belong together.
**Reading and Thinking** Drawing Conclusions (1): Have your child complete the sentence by writing a check beside the correct answer.
Predicting Outcomes (2): Have your child read the question and, based on the story events, write a check beside the correct answer.
**Learning to Study** Alphabetical Order (1-4): Have your child write each set of letters in alphabetical order.

# The Tea Party

When Little Critter got home, he put the kittens in the clubhouse. Mrs. Jones would be coming soon to see if the mother cat was hers.

Little Sister was in the clubhouse. The mother cat was wearing a dress. Little Sister was having a tea party.

"Hi," said Little Sister. "Want a cup of tea?"

"Okay," said Little Critter. "You really love this cat, don't you?"

"I wish she were mine," said Little Sister.

"A lady is coming soon," said Little Critter. "This may be her cat."

Little Sister pouted. "I hope not!"

## Reading and Thinking

1. Little Sister was having a

   ____ game. ____ party. ____ meal.

2. What was the mother cat wearing?

   ____ a collar

   ____ socks

   ____ a dress

## Working with Words

| 1. | 2. | 3. |
|---|---|---|
| pout<br>shout  | dress<br>drink  | cup<br>cry  |

4. We saw two ______________ at the farm.

5. The kittens had brown ______________.

6. One ______________ was just a baby.

7. Its ______________ was not very long.

| kitten |
|---|
| kittens |
| tail |
| tails |

**Reading and Thinking** Picture Clues (1): Have your child look at the picture that accompanies the story, then complete the unfinished sentence by writing a check beside the correct answer. Predicting Outcomes (2): Have your child read the question and, based on the story events, write a check beside the correct answer.
**Working with Words** Consonant Digraphs (1-3): Have your child name each picture and circle the word that names or best describes it. Singular and Plural (4-7): Have your child read the sentences and the words in the small box, then choose the word that makes sense in each sentence, and write it in the blank.

# A Home for All

Mrs. Jones came to the Critter's house. The mother cat was her cat, Patches. Mrs. Jones was happy to have her back.

"I am glad we found her owner," said Mrs. Critter.

"Thank you for taking care of Patches and her kittens," said Mrs. Jones.

"We found homes for all of the kittens," said Mr. Critter.

Little Critter looked surprised. "Where are they going to live?"

"Grandma and Grandpa are going to keep them on the farm. The farm has places for kittens to run and play," said Mrs. Critter.

Little Critter was glad. He knew he could always visit the kittens at Grandma and Grandpa's farm.

## Reading and Thinking

1. Look at the story picture. Patches' fur was

   ____ black. ____ orange. ____ black and orange.

2. ____ Mrs. Critter was glad to find Patches' owner.

   ____ Mrs. Jones said thank you.

   ____ Mrs. Jones came over.

3. His dog got a ______________ at the pet show.

   play prize right

4. Dad helped me ______________ the horse.

   into only onto

## Working with Words

| 1. | 2. | 3. |
|---|---|---|
| farm<br>frog | glad<br>glass 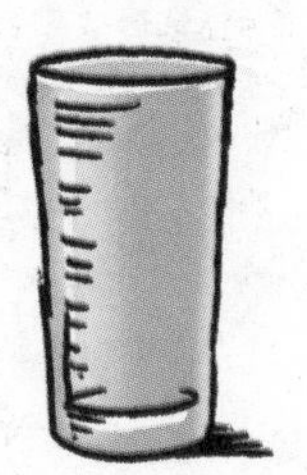 | tail<br>tell  |

I'll that's let's don't

4. that is ______________
5. I will ______________
6. let us ______________
7. do not ______________

**Reading and Thinking** Picture Clues (1): Have your child look at the picture that accompanies the story, then complete the unfinished sentence by writing a check beside the correct answer. Sequence (2): Have your child read the sentences and number them to show the order of events in the story. Context Clues (3-4): Have your child read each sentence and write the word that best completes it.
**Working with Words** Vowel Digraphs and Diphthongs (1-3): Have your child name each picture and circle the word that names or best describes it. Contractions (4-7): Have your child read the contractions at the top of the exercise, then read each numbered pair of words. Have your child write the contraction for the two words in the blank.

# Cheer Up, Little Sister

The Critter family said good-bye to Patches and Mrs. Jones.

Little Sister was unhappy. She hid under her bed.

The mother cat was gone. Soon the kittens would be gone too. Who would she have tea parties with now?

Little Critter tried to make Little Sister feel better. He sang a song, but Little Sister plugged her ears. He did a funny dance, but it made her cry. He did a cartwheel, but he crashed into the wall. He brought dinner to her room, but he spilled peas and carrots on the floor.

"Cheer up, Little Sister!" said Little Critter.

# Knowing the Words

1. eyes ears think nose
2. grumpy little unhappy angry

# Reading and Thinking

1. Little Sister was feeling
   ____ sad. ____ happy. ____ angry.
2. We are going to the farm ________________.
   today told turned

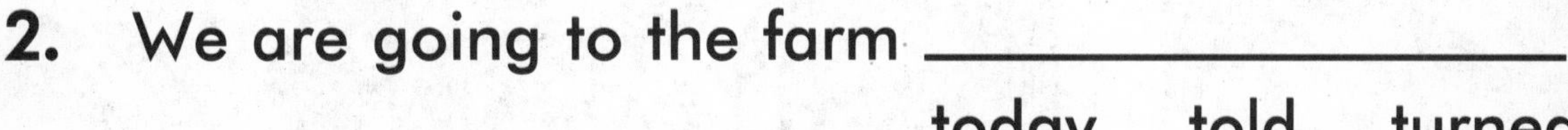

3. A ______________ would not make a good pet.
   cat dog lion

# Working with Words

1. Malcolm threw a ball into the _____________.
   air are
2. Will you read us a story _____________?
   new now
3. Do you _____________ the circus?
   saw see

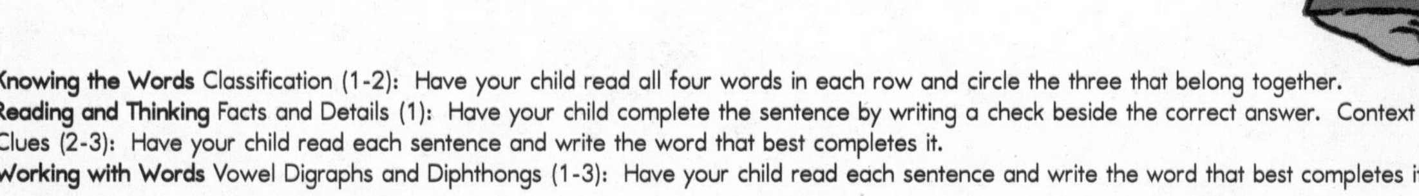

**Knowing the Words** Classification (1-2): Have your child read all four words in each row and circle the three that belong together.
**Reading and Thinking** Facts and Details (1): Have your child complete the sentence by writing a check beside the correct answer. Context Clues (2-3): Have your child read each sentence and write the word that best completes it.
**Working with Words** Vowel Digraphs and Diphthongs (1-3): Have your child read each sentence and write the word that best completes it.

# Missing Kittens

It was early Saturday morning and time to leave for Grandma and Grandpa's.

"I'll go get the kittens, Mom," said Little Critter.

Little Critter looked in the clubhouse where the kittens slept. No kittens. Little Critter looked in the garage. No kittens. He checked the yard.
No kittens.

Mrs. Critter said, "Little Critter, have you seen Little Sister?"

"No. But I bet she is with the kittens!"

They went to Little Sister's room. She wasn't in her bed. Little Critter opened the closet. Little Sister was sitting on a pile of pillows and blankets with the four kittens.

She cried, "I don't want the kittens to go!"

# Reading and Thinking

1. Why did Little Sister hide with the kittens?

   ____ She was cold.

   ____ She wanted to keep the kittens.

   ____ The kittens were playing.

2. This story is about

   ____ hiding in the closet.

   ____ running away.

   ____ going to the zoo.

# Working with Words

1. I h___p___ you get a pr___z___ for your picture.

2. H___ asked me to let him r___d___ the horse.

3. W___ will t___k___ some flowers to Mr. Molini.

---

4. I am ______________ you a happy day.

   wished   wishing

5. I ______________ the covers over my head.

   pulls   pulled

**Reading and Thinking** Drawing Conclusions (1): Have your child read the question and write a check beside the correct answer. Main Idea (2): Have your child complete the sentence by writing a check beside the correct answer.
**Working with Words** Long Vowels (1-3): Have your child read each sentence, then complete each unfinished word by writing the missing letters. Base Words and Endings (4-5): Have your child read each sentence and write the word that correctly completes it.

# A Funny Car Ride

Little Critter and his family got in the car and buckled their seatbelts. The kittens were in a box in the back seat.

"Meow! Meow! Meow!" they cried.

"Little Critter, should we let the kittens out of the box? They are crying so much," said Mrs. Critter.

Little Critter lifted the lid of the box. The kittens peeked out and sniffed around the car.

Two kittens curled up on Mr. Critter's lap. Another kitten settled on Mr. Critter's shoulder. The last kitten wanted to sit on Mr. Critter's head.

"Help! These kittens are crawling all over me!" cried Mr. Critter.

Little Critter laughed. His dad could not start the car with the kittens climbing on him.

"Here, Kitties!" called Little Critter. "Get back into your box."

The kittens climbed back in their box.

"Thanks, Little Critter," said Dad. "Now I can drive the car!"

## Knowing the Words

| | | | | |
|---|---|---|---|---|
| 1. | jumping | throwing | sleep | running |
| 2. | words | story | book | box |
| 3. | maybe | Mr. | Ms. | Mrs. |
| 4. | shoulder | head | arm | car |

## Reading and Thinking

1. This story takes place in the

____ farm. ____ zoo. ____ car.

2. Who was not in the car with Little Critter?

____ Little Sister. ____ Mrs. Critter. ____ Grandma

## Learning to Study

1. car arm box

2. kitten little jump

**Knowing the Words** Classification (1-4): Have your child read all four words in each row and circle the three that belong together.
**Reading and Thinking** Drawing Conclusions (1): Have your child complete the sentence by writing a check beside the correct answer. Facts and Details (2): Have your child read the question and write a check beside the correct answer.
**Learning to Study** Alphabetical Order (1-2): Have your child read each set of words and write them in alphabetical order.

# Moooooooo!

Little Critter was excited to be visiting his grandparents at the farm. He jumped out of the car. The kittens followed him.

Little Critter hugged his grandparents.

"What sweet kittens!" said Grandma. "There is lots of room for them to run here."

Little Critter followed the kittens into the barn. Some cows were there eating hay.

One kitten ran between a cow's legs.

"Oh, no!" said Little Critter. "The cow might step on the kitten!"

Little Critter dove after the kitten.

"MOO!" went the cow right in Little Critter's face.

Grandpa laughed. "Little Critter, that kitten can take care of herself!"

## Reading and Thinking

1. Where did the kitten go?

   ____ into the house.

   ____ into the barn.

   ____ under the fence.

2. Mr. Critter ______________ some money in his pocket.

   found friend

3. The man likes to read ______________ he eats lunch.

   while will

## Working with Words

| ch |
|---|
| sh |
| th |
| wh |

1. She will ____ow the dog a new trick.
2. I watched their baby ____ile they were gone.
3. ____ose ____ildren go to my school.

---

4. __________ buy a balloon for Malcolm.

   I will

5. We __________ make it to the bus stop on time.

   did not

**Reading and Thinking** Predicting Outcomes (1): Have your child read the question and based on the story events, write a check beside the correct answer. Context Clues (2-3): Have your child read each sentence and write the word that best completes it.
**Working with Words** Consonant Digraphs (1-3): Have your child read each sentence, then complete each unfinished word by writing the missing letters. Point out that sentence 3 should begin with a capital letter. Contractions (4-5): Have your child read each sentence with the two words below the blank. In the blank, have your child write the contraction for the words.

# A Quiet Place

Little Critter and the kittens wandered around the farm. The chickens were running around their coop. The kittens did not want the chickens to peck them. Neither did Little Critter.

The pigs were rolling around in the mud. The kittens did not like the smell of the pigpen. Neither did Little Critter!

The kittens followed Little Critter into the sheep barn. The sheep were resting in their stalls. The tired kittens curled up in the hay for a nap. So did Little Critter.

Little Critter woke up. Something wet was licking his face. It was Shep, the farm dog!

"I guess my nap is over," said Little Critter.

## Reading and Thinking

1\. ____ Little Critter fell asleep.

____ Little Critter went to the sheep barn.

____ Little Critter went to the chicken coop.

2\. This story is about

____ a funny sheep.

____ a place to nap.

____ a big lunch.

## Working with Words

1\. H___ will w___k___ up soon.

2\. A m___l___ looks a little l___k___ a horse.

---

3\. A sheep ______________ grass.

eats eating

4\. I laughed when Malcolm ______________ me.

tricks tricked

5\. I can hear Dad ______________ me.

called calling

**Reading and Thinking** Sequence (1): Have your child read the sentences and number them to show the order of events in the story. Main Idea (2): Have your child complete the sentence by writing a check beside the correct answer.
**Working with Words** Long Vowels (1-2): Have your child read each sentence, then complete each unfinished word by writing the missing letters. Base Words and Endings (3-5): Have your child read each sentence and write the word that correctly completes it.

# Little Critter's Idea

Little Critter had a wonderful day at the farm. He visited all the animals. He played tag with the goats. He rode in the tree swing in the yard. He ate the big, yummy lunch that Grandma made.

Little Sister did only one thing. She spent the whole day petting her favorite orange kitten.

Little Critter went inside to talk to his mom and dad.

"Mom and Dad, do you think we could keep one kitten for Little Sister? She is so sad."

"You are right, Little Critter. She is sad," said Mr. Critter.

"We could surprise her," said Little Critter. "Grandma and Grandpa can help."

# Reading and Thinking

1. Little Critter had

   ____ a big breakfast.

   ____ a fun day.

   ____ a bad dream.

2. Why did Little Critter want to surprise Little Sister?

______________________________________________

______________________________________________

# Working with Words

| 1. | 2. | 3. |
|---|---|---|
| c_a_t | g___t | c___n |
| f_a_t | l___t | f___n |
| h_a_t | w___t | m___n |

4. read ride

5. book boxes

6. sneeze snow

**Reading and Thinking** Facts and Details (1): Have your child complete the sentence by writing a check beside the correct answer. Cause and Effect (2): Have your child read the question and write the answer in the blanks.
**Working with Words** Short Vowels, Rhyming Words (1-3): Using the completed item as an example, have your child form rhyming words in each column by writing the same vowel in each blank. Vowel Digraphs and Diphthongs (4-6): Have your child name each picture and circle the word that names or best describes it.

# A Surprise for Little Sister

Little Sister said good-bye to the kittens. She hugged the orange kitten for a long time. Then Little Critter and his family got into their car to go home.

Mr. Critter began to drive away. Suddenly, Grandma called after them.

"You forgot something! You forgot something!" she called.

Little Critter rolled down his window. Grandma handed the orange kitten to him. He placed the kitten on Little Sister's lap.

"We get to keep her?" asked Little Sister.

"No, you get to keep her," said Little Critter. "The orange kitten is your cat."

"Don't worry, Little Critter," said Little Sister. "I'll share. I am going to call her Tangerine, because she is orange."

## Knowing the Words

1. flowers grass boxes tree
2. table bed desk window
3. boy she uncle man

## Reading and Thinking

1. Who helped Little Critter surprise Little Sister?

______________________________

2. Tangerine has ________ fur.

___ green ___ orange ___ spotted

## Learning to Study

1. goat horse funny

_______________

_______________

_______________

2. rose table shoe

_______________

_______________

_______________

**Knowing the Words** Classification (1-3): Have your child read all four words in each row and circle the three that belong together.
**Reading and Thinking** Facts and Details (1): Have your child read the question and write the answer in the blank. Picture Clues (2): Have your child look at the picture that accompanies the story, then complete the unfinished sentence by writing a check beside the correct answer.
**Learning to Study** Alphabetical Order(1-2): Have your child read each set of words and write them in alphabetical order.

# Back Home

Little Critter's family was happy to be home after a long day at the farm.

"All the kittens have good homes," said Little Critter.

"Mr. Molini has Stripe, Maurice and Molly have Speckle and Freckle, Grandma and Grandpa have three new farm kittens, and Little Sister has Tangerine."

Little Critter stopped talking. His mom had fallen asleep in a chair. His dad was asleep on the couch. Little Sister was asleep on the floor.

Tangerine was looking at something out the window.

"What is it, Tangerine?" asked Little Critter.

Little Critter looked out and saw a small dog. He had no collar. He was very skinny and dirty.

Little Critter opened the door. He said to the dog, "You look like you are lost."

# Reading and Thinking

1. What did Little Critter do when he saw the dog?

   ____ He fell asleep.

   ____ He opened the door.

   ____ He woke up Little Sister.

2. Do you think Little Critter will help the dog?

   __________ Why or why not? ____________________

   ________________________________________

# Working with Words

1. Molly and I are in the s__m__ room at school.
2. I h__p__ Maurice will wr__t__ to me.
3. What t__m__ does the bus stop here?

---

4. can not __________
5. let us __________
6. that is __________
7. I will __________

**Reading and Thinking** Facts and Details (1): Have your child read the question and write a check beside the correct answer. Predicting Outcomes (2): Have your child read the questions and, based on the story events and his or her own opinion, write the answers in the blanks.
**Working with Words** Long Vowels (1-3): Have your child read each sentence, then complete each unfinished word by writing the missing letters. Contractions (4-7): Have your child read the two words beside each blank. In the blank, have your child write the contraction for the words.

# Practice Page

 **Directions:** Have your child use this page for extra practice.

1. gr

gr grapes | puppy | gr grass

2. a hat e — (a)
3. i pig u — (i)
4. o cup u — (u)
5. a bed e — (e)
6. i doll o — (o)
7. a dog o — (o)

8.

3 | 2 | 1

**Blends (1):** Review the sound of the blend **gr**. Have your child name each picture, then write **gr** below each picture whose name begins with the **gr** sound. Have your child put an X directly on the picture that does not begin with the **gr** sound.
**Short Vowels (2-7):** Have your child name each picture and listen to the vowel sound, then circle the correct vowel below the picture.
**Sequence (8):** Have your child look at all three pictures, then write **1** below the event that would happen first, **2** below the event that would happen second, and **3** below the event that would happen third.

5

1. b bell
2. f fence
3. s sun

4. pr

pr present | pr prize | heart

5. in (over) under on

6. in over (under) on

**Initial Consonants (1-3):** Have your child name each picture, listen to the beginning sound, and write the beginning letter below the picture.
**Blends (4):** Review the sound of the blend **pr**. Have your child name each picture, then write **pr** below each picture whose name begins with the **pr** sound. Have your child put an X directly on the picture that does not begin with the **pr** sound.
**Picture Clues (5-6):** Ask your child to read the words in each box and circle the word that best describes where the puppy is.

7

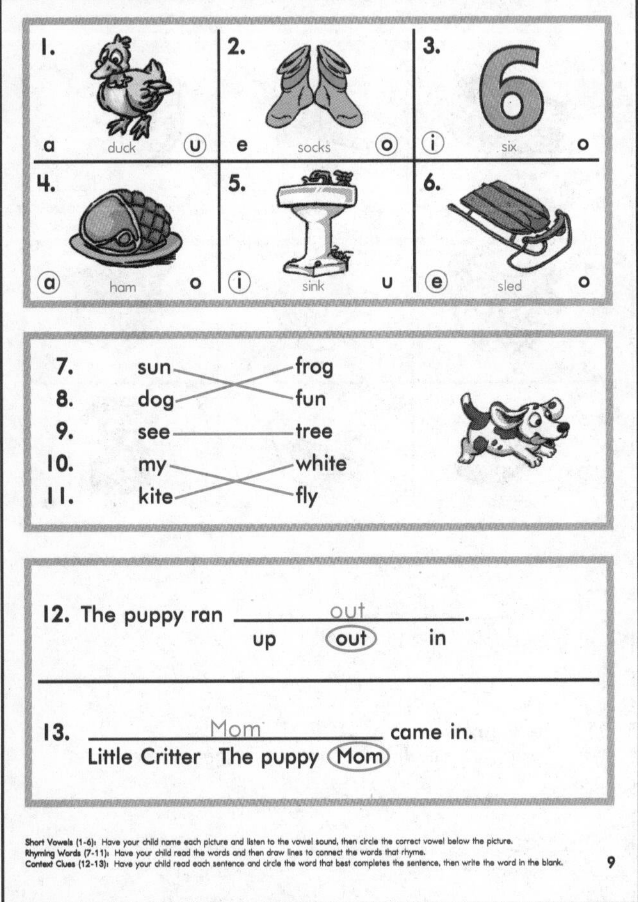

1. a duck u — (u)
2. e socks o — (o)
3. i six o — (i)
4. a ham o — (a)
5. i sink u — (i)
6. e sled o — (e)

7. sun — fun
8. dog — frog
9. see — tree
10. my — fly
11. kite — white

12. The puppy ran out.
up (out) in

13. Mom came in.
Little Critter The puppy (Mom)

**Short Vowels (1-6):** Have your child name each picture and listen to the vowel sound, then circle the correct vowel below the picture.
**Rhyming Words (7-11):** Have your child read the words and then draw lines to connect the words that rhyme.
**Context Clues (12-13):** Have your child read each sentence and circle the word that best completes the sentence, then write the word in the blank.

9

1. l ladder
2. j jack-in-the-box
3. r radio

4. n balloon
5. l pencil
6. s gas

7. (There are two.)
There are three.

8. It is pretty.
(It is not pretty.)

**Initial Consonants (1-3):** Have your child name each picture, listen to the beginning sound, and write the beginning letter below the picture.
**Final Consonants (4-6):** Have your child name each picture, listen to the ending sound, and write the ending letter below the picture.
**Picture Clues (7-8):** Ask your child to read the sentences in each box and circle the sentence that best describes the picture.

11

1\. n nail  2. t top  3. d dog

4\. e ten o  5. a nut u  6. i fish u

7\. i mop o  8. a fan e  9. o fox u

10\.
Little Critter plays in the grass.
He sees something coming.
It cannot go fast.
What is it?
a squirrel
a turtle
a house

11\.
The puppy plays in the grass.
A turtle comes near.
The puppy cannot see it.
Where is the turtle?
on a ball
in back of the puppy
under the snow

**Initial Consonants (1-3):** Have your child name each picture, listen to the beginning sound, and write the beginning letter below the picture.
**Short Vowels (4-9):** Have your child name each picture and listen to the vowel sound, then circle the correct vowel below the picture.
**Drawing Conclusions (10-11):** Have your child read the sentences in each box, then circle the phrase that makes the most sense.

13

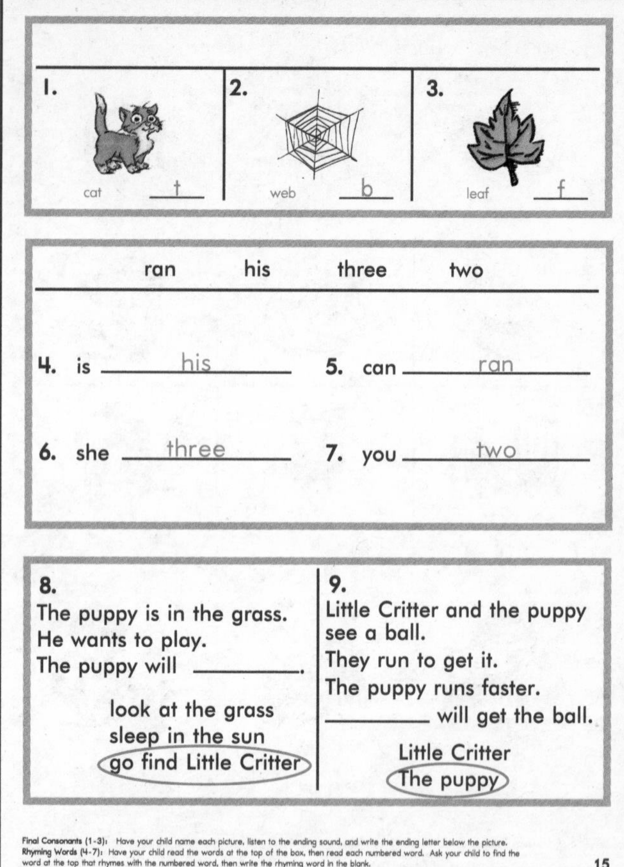

1\. cat t  2. web b  3. leaf f

ran his three two

4\. is his  5. can ran

6\. she three  7. you two

8\.
The puppy is in the grass.
He wants to play.
The puppy will ______.
look at the grass
sleep in the sun
go find Little Critter

9\.
Little Critter and the puppy see a ball.
They run to get it.
The puppy runs faster.
______ will get the ball.
Little Critter
The puppy

**Final Consonants (1-3):** Have your child name each picture, listen to the ending sound, and write the ending letter below the picture.
**Rhyming Words (4-7):** Have your child read the words at the top of the box, then read each numbered word. Ask your child to find the word at the top that rhymes with the numbered word, then write the rhyming word in the blank.
**Predicting Outcomes (8-9):** Have your child read the sentences in each box, then circle the phrase or word below that makes sense.

15

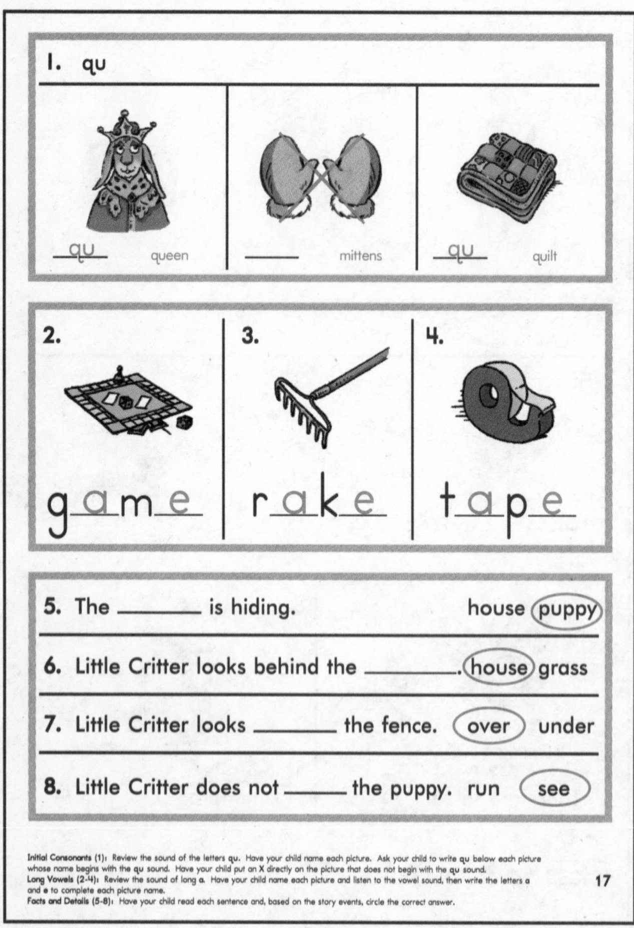

1\. qu

qu queen  mittens  qu quilt

2\. game  3. rake  4. tape

5\. The ______ is hiding. house puppy

6\. Little Critter looks behind the ______. house grass

7\. Little Critter looks ______ the fence. over under

8\. Little Critter does not ______ the puppy. run see

**Initial Consonants (1):** Review the sound of the letters **qu**. Have your child name each picture. Ask your child to write **qu** below each picture whose name begins with the **qu** sound. Have your child put an X directly on the picture that does not begin with the **qu** sound.
**Long Vowels (2-4):** Review the sound of long **a**. Have your child name each picture and listen to the vowel sound, then write the letters **a** and **e** to complete each picture name.
**Facts and Details (5-8):** Have your child read each sentence and, based on the story events, circle the correct answer.

17

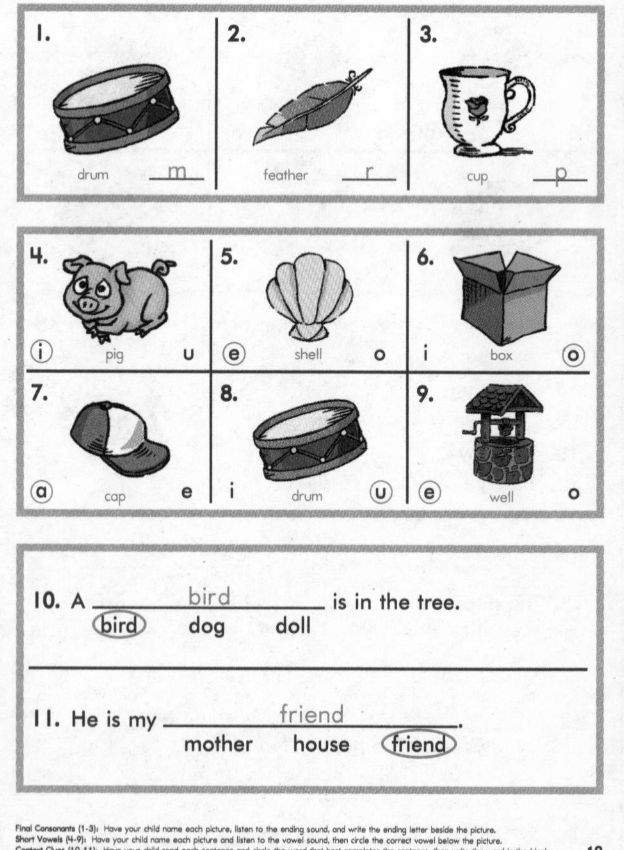

1\. drum m  2. feather r  3. cup p

4\. i pig u  5. e shell o  6. i box o

7\. a cap e  8. i drum u  9. e well o

10\. A bird is in the tree.
bird dog doll

11\. He is my friend.
mother house friend

**Final Consonants (1-3):** Have your child name each picture, listen to the ending sound, and write the ending letter beside the picture.
**Short Vowels (4-9):** Have your child name each picture and listen to the vowel sound, then circle the correct vowel below the picture.
**Context Clues (10-11):** Have your child read each sentence and circle the word that best completes the sentence, then write the word in the blank.

19

1. fr

butterfly | fr frog | fr frame

don't isn't can't

isn't

2. is not isn't

3. do not don't

4. can not can't

5.
The water comes out.
It goes everywhere.
Little Critter runs away.
He __________ water.

likes doesn't like

6.
It is something that jumps.
It likes water.
It can't run fast.
It is a __________.

duck frog dog

**Blends (1):** Review the sound of the blend **fr**. Have your child name each picture, then write **fr** below each picture whose name begins with the **fr** sound. Have your child put an X directly on the picture that does not begin with the **fr** sound.
**Contractions (2-4):** Explain the concept of contractions to your child, then read the contractions at the top of the box. Have your child read each numbered pair of words, then write the contraction for the two words in the blank.
**Drawing Conclusions (5-6):** Have your child read the sentences in each box, then circle the word or phrase that makes the most sense.

21

1. kite 2. fire 3. bike

4.

5.

6. birds friend nest tree

7.
"Get down, Puppy!"
"You are wet, Puppy."

8.
"Go up there."
"Come down here!"

**Long Vowels (1-3):** Review the sound of long **i**. Have your child name each picture and listen to the vowel sound, then write the letters **i** and **e** to complete each picture name.
**Classification (4-6):** Have your child look at all four pictures or words in each row and circle the three that belong together.
**Picture Clues (7-8):** Ask your child to look at the picture and read the sentences in each box, then circle the sentence that your child would say to the puppy.

23

1. bed d 2. dress s 3. can n

4. gate 5. five 6. lake



7.
Little Critter sees something run under the table.
He wants to see what it is.
What will Little Critter do?

play with a friend
get some hot water
look under the table

8.
The frog plays in the sun.
The frog is hot.
What will the frog do?

jump into cold water
jump up and down
sleep in the sun

**Final Consonants (1-3):** Have your child name each picture, listen to the ending sound, and write the ending letter below the picture.
**Long Vowels (4-6):** Have your child name each picture and listen to the vowel sound, then write the letters that complete the picture name.
**Predicting Outcomes (7-8):** Have your child read the sentences in each box, then circle the phrase below that makes sense.

25

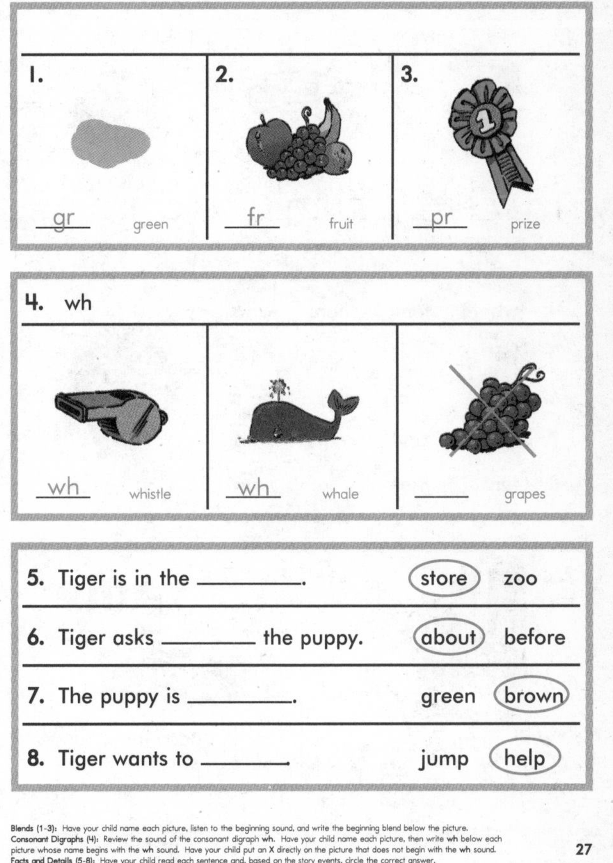

1. gr green 2. fr fruit 3. pr prize

4. wh

wh whistle | wh whale | grapes

5. Tiger is in the __________. store zoo

6. Tiger asks __________ the puppy. about before

7. The puppy is __________. green brown

8. Tiger wants to __________. jump help

**Blends (1-3):** Have your child name each picture, listen to the beginning sound, and write the beginning blend below the picture.
**Consonant Digraphs (4):** Review the sound of the consonant digraph **wh**. Have your child name each picture, then write **wh** below each picture whose name begins with the **wh** sound. Have your child put an X directly on the picture that does not begin with the **wh** sound.
**Facts and Details (5-8):** Have your child read each sentence and, based on the story events, circle the correct answer.

27

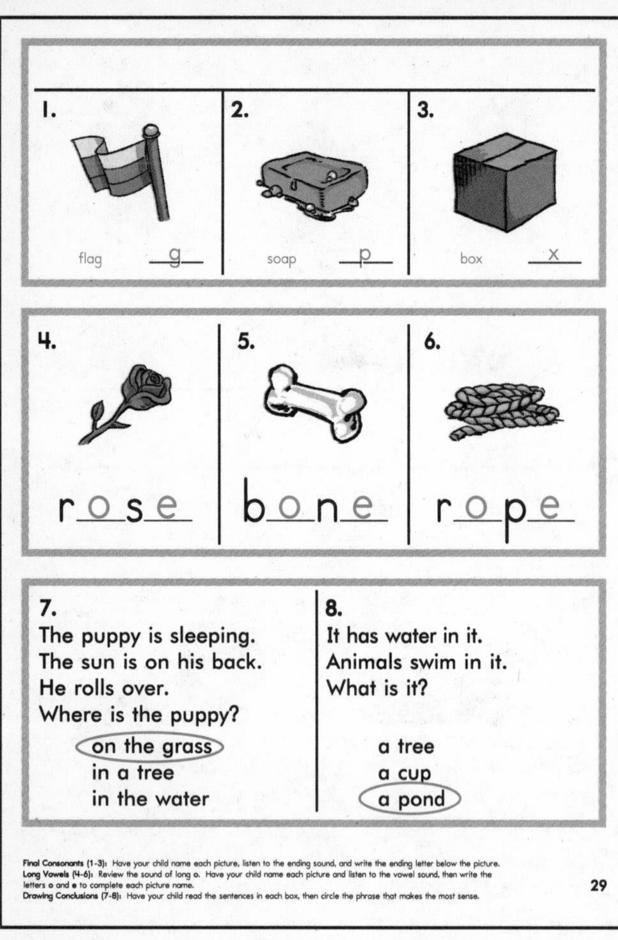

1. flag g
2. soap p
3. box x

4. rose
5. bone
6. rope

7. The puppy is sleeping.
The sun is on his back.
He rolls over.
Where is the puppy?
on the grass
in a tree
in the water

8. It has water in it.
Animals swim in it.
What is it?
a tree
a cup
a pond

**Final Consonants (1-3):** Have your child name each picture, listen to the ending sound, and write the ending letter below the picture.
**Long Vowels (4-6):** Review the sound of long o. Have your child name each picture and listen to the vowel sound, then write the letters o and e to complete each picture name.
**Drawing Conclusions (7-8):** Have your child read the sentences in each box, then circle the phrase that makes the most sense.

29

1. th

th thermometer
th thumb
game

2. Do you ______ to play?
want wants wanted

3. Little Critter ______ with a ball.
play plays playing

4. Little Critter is ______ for the puppy.
looks looked looking

5. The frog has ______.
jumps jumped jumping

6.
2 3 1

**Consonant Digraphs (1):** Review the sound of the consonant digraph **th**. Have your child name each picture, then write **th** below each picture whose name begins with the **th** sound. Have your child put an **X** directly on the picture that does not begin with the **th** sound.
**Base Words and Endings (2-5):** Have your child read each sentence and circle the word that correctly completes the sentence.
**Sequence (6):** Have your child look at all three pictures, then write **1** below the event that would happen first, **2** below the event that would happen second, and **3** below the event that would happen third.

31

1. mule
2. tune
3. cube

| | | | | |
|---|---|---|---|---|
| 4. | **where** | tent | there | who |
| 5. | **hot** | not | her | new |
| 6. | **stop** | sun | play | pop |
| 7. | **some** | cold | come | said |
| 8. | **tent** | them | went | want |

9.
"Walk here, Puppy."
"Don't walk in here."

10.
"You can sleep here, Puppy."
"You can eat here."

**Long Vowels (1-3):** Review the sound of long u. Have your child name each picture and listen to the vowel sound, then write the letters u and e to complete each picture name.
**Rhyming Words (4-8):** Have your child read the words in each row, then circle the word that rhymes with the first word in each row.
**Picture Clues (9-10):** Ask your child to look at the picture and read sentences in each box, then circle the sentence that your child would say to the puppy.

33

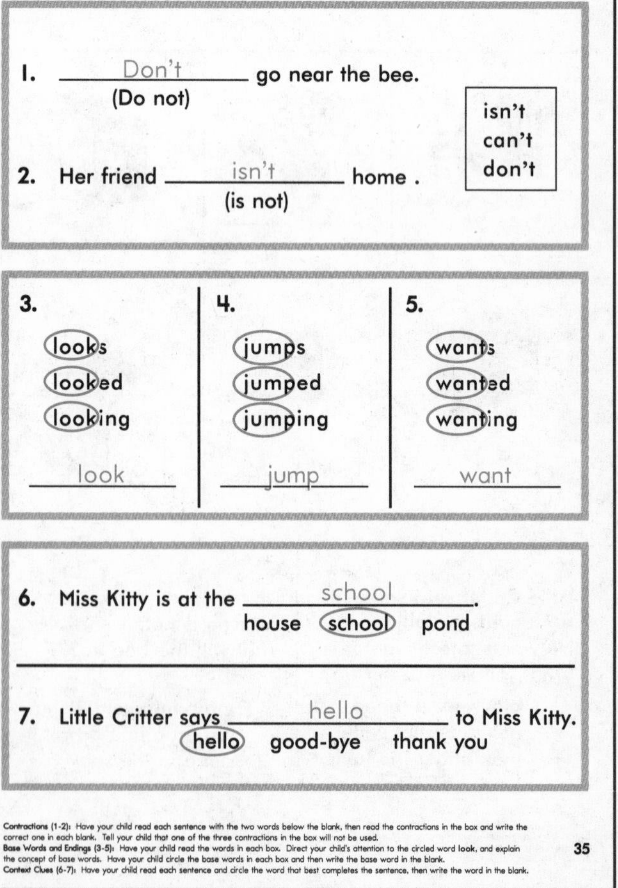

1. Don't go near the bee.
(Do not)

2. Her friend isn't home.
(is not)

isn't
can't
don't

3. looks looked looking — look
4. jumps jumped jumping — jump
5. wants wanted wanting — want

6. Miss Kitty is at the school.
house school pond

7. Little Critter says hello to Miss Kitty.
hello good-bye thank you

**Contractions (1-2):** Have your child read each sentence with the two words below the blank, then read the contractions in the box and write the correct one in each blank. Tell your child that one of the three contractions in the box will not be used.
**Base Words and Endings (3-5):** Have your child read the words in each box. Direct your child's attention to the circled word **look**, and explain the concept of base words. Have your child circle the base words in each box and then write the base word in the blank.
**Context Clues (6-7):** Have your child read each sentence and circle the word that best completes the sentence, then write the word in the blank.

35

1. wh wheel
2. th thirteen
3. wh whistle

4. hose
5. mule
6. robe

7. This is a home for the puppy.
This is a home for birds.

8. It is hot out here.
It is cold out here.

**Consonant Digraphs (1-3):** Have your child name each picture, listen to the beginning sound, and write the beginning consonant digraph in the blank below the picture.
**Long Vowels (4-6):** Have your child name each picture and listen to the vowel sound, then write the letters that complete the picture name.
**Picture Clues (7-8):** Ask your child to read the sentences in each box and circle the sentence that best describes the picture.

37

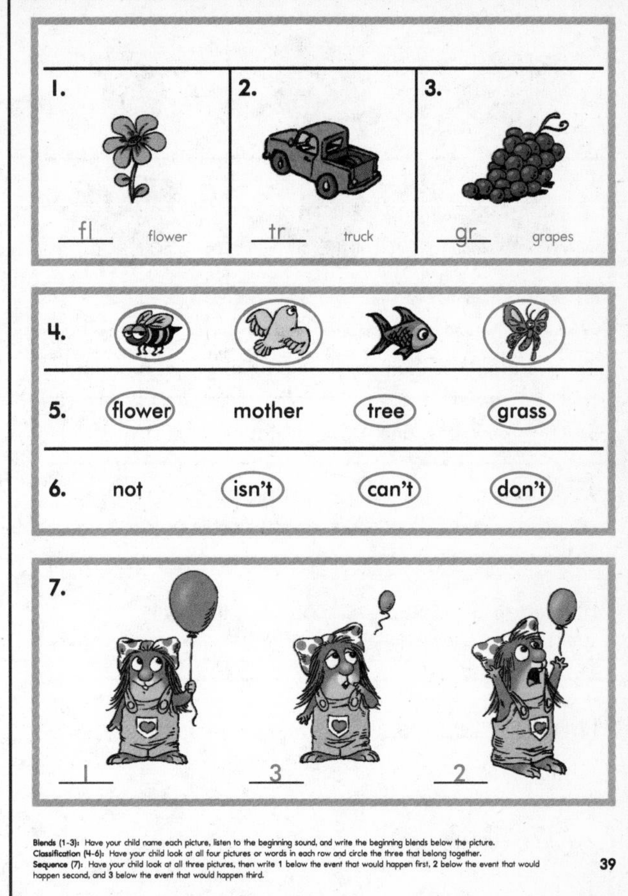

1. fl flower
2. tr truck
3. gr grapes

4.

5. flower mother tree grass

6. not isn't can't don't

7. 1 3 2

**Blends (1-3):** Have your child name each picture, listen to the beginning sound, and write the beginning blends below the picture.
**Classification (4-6):** Have your child look at all four pictures or words in each row and circle the three that belong together.
**Sequence (7):** Have your child look at all three pictures, then write **1** below the event that would happen first, **2** below the event that would happen second, and **3** below the event that would happen third.

39

1. sh

camel
sh shoe
sh shirt

2. Little Critter has ______ running.
stop stops stopped

3. A squirrel ______ down the tree.
come comes coming

4. The puppy is ______ very fast.
run runs running

5. I don't ______ that bee.
like likes liked

6. The puppy jumps and plays.
He runs fast.
He gets tired.
What will he do next?
run faster
play tag
go to sleep

7. Little Critter and the puppy are playing.
A bee is coming. It is something they do not like.
What will they do next?
run away
play with the bee
run at the bee

**Consonant Digraphs (1):** Review the sound of the consonant digraph **sh**. Have your child name each picture, then write **sh** below each picture whose name begins with the **sh** sound. Have your child put an **X** directly on the picture that does not begin with the **sh** sound.
**Base Words and Endings (2-5):** Have your child read each sentence and circle the word that correctly completes the sentence.
**Predicting Outcomes (6-7):** Have your child read the sentences in each box, then circle the phrase below that makes sense.

41

1. st stamp
2. pr present
3. sn snail

4. Where is Little Critter?
He is in his room.

5. Where is Little Sister?
She is not here.

6. They are good to play with.
You cannot play with them.

7. They are good to walk on.
Do not walk on them.

**Blends (1-3):** Have your child name each picture, listen to the beginning sound, and write the beginning blend in the blank below the picture.
**Long Vowels (4-5):** Review the sound of long **e**. Have your child read each item and decide what the incomplete word should be. Have your child write the letter **e** to complete the word.
**Picture Clues (6-7):** Direct your child to read the sentences in each box and circle the sentence that best describes the picture.

43

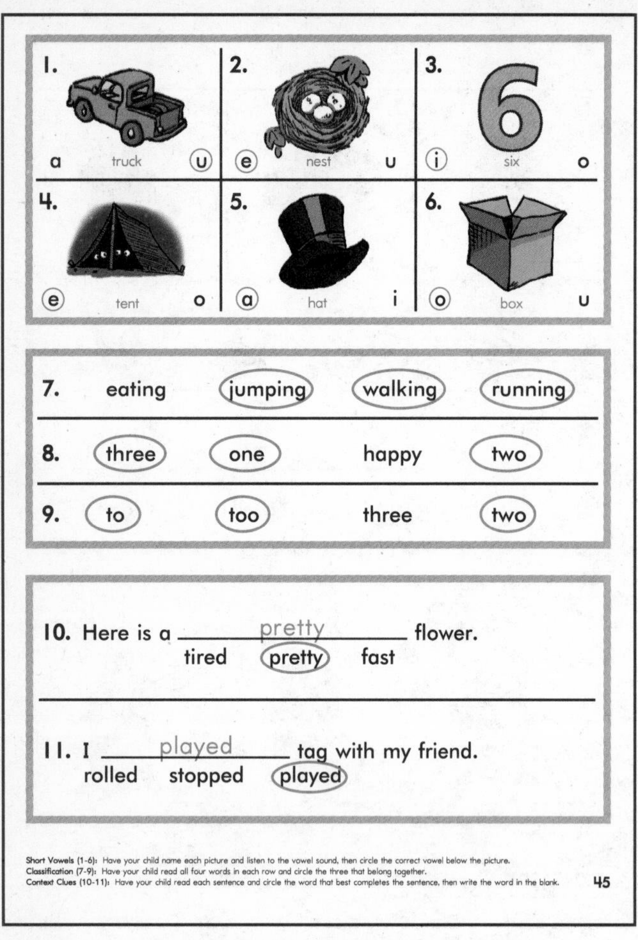

1\. a truck u e

2\. e nest u

3\. i six o

4\. e tent o

5\. a hat i

6\. o box u

7\. eating jumping walking running

8\. three one happy two

9\. to too three two

10\. Here is a pretty flower.
tired pretty fast

11\. I played tag with my friend.
rolled stopped played

**Short Vowels (1-6):** Have your child name each picture and listen to the vowel sound, then circle the correct vowel below the picture.
**Classification (7-9):** Have your child read all four words in each row and circle the three that belong together.
**Context Clues (10-11):** Have your child read each sentence and circle the word that best completes the sentence, then write the word in the blank.

45

1\. kite

2\. wave

3\. note

other bee try day

4\. fly try

5\. play day

6\. mother other

7\. tree bee

8\. The puppy is in the ______. yard house

9\. Little Critter ______ the puppy. holds sees

10\. The puppy digs ______ the flowers. up down

11\. The puppy ______ muddy. is runs

**Long Vowels (1-3):** Have your child name each picture and listen to the vowel sound, then write the letters that complete the picture name.
**Rhyming Words (4-7):** Have your child read the words at the top of the box, then read each numbered word. Ask your child to find the word at the top that rhymes with the numbered word, then write the rhyming word in the blank.
**Facts and Details (8-11):** Have your child read each sentence and, based on the story events, circle the correct answer.

47

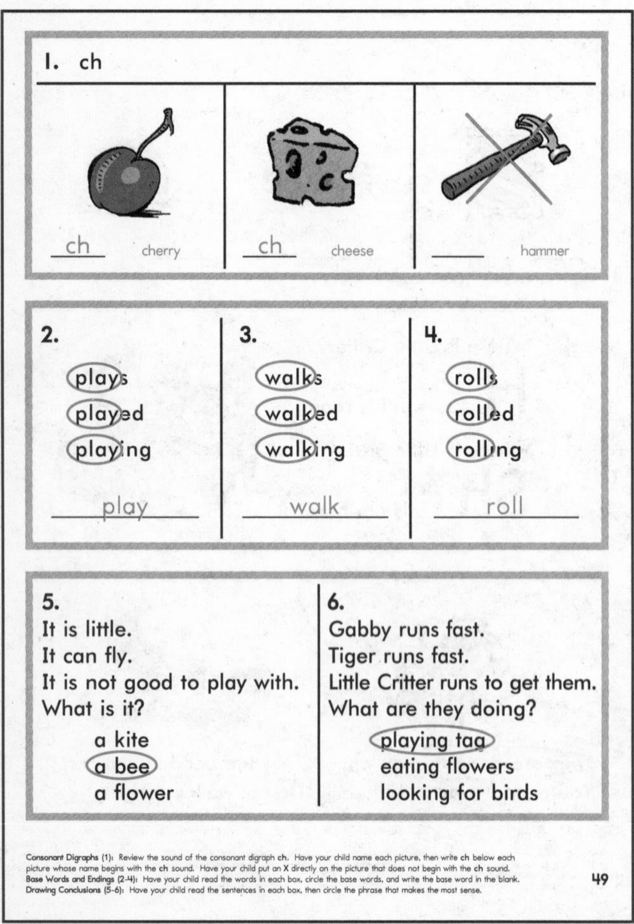

1\. ch

ch cherry

ch cheese

hammer

2\.
plays
played
playing
play

3\.
walks
walked
walking
walk

4\.
rolls
rolled
rolling
roll

5\.
It is little.
It can fly.
It is not good to play with.
What is it?
a kite
a bee
a flower

6\.
Gabby runs fast.
Tiger runs fast.
Little Critter runs to get them.
What are they doing?
playing tag
eating flowers
looking for birds

**Consonant Digraphs (1):** Review the sound of the consonant digraph **ch**. Have your child name each picture, then write **ch** below each picture whose name begins with the **ch** sound. Have your child put an **X** directly on the picture that does not begin with the **ch** sound.
**Base Words and Endings (2-4):** Have your child read the words in each box, circle the base words, and write the base word in the blank.
**Drawing Conclusions (5-6):** Have your child read the sentences in each box, then circle the phrase that makes the most sense.

49

1\. fr fruit

2\. sl slide

3\. pl plant

4\. do not don't

5\. was not wasn't

6\. is not isn't

7\. did not didn't

8\. 3 1 2

**Blends (1-3):** Have your child name each picture, listen to the beginning sound, and write the beginning blend below the picture.
**Contractions (4-7):** Have your child read the two words beside each blank, then write the contraction for the words in the blank.
**Sequence (8):** Have your child look at all three pictures, then write **1** below the event that would happen first, **2** below the event that would happen second, and **3** below the event that would happen third.

51

1. sh shell
2. ch chain
3. sh ship

4. tune
5. nine
6. cane

7. Mom ______ the puppy. (pets) walks
8. Dad gives him a ______ bone. (big) blue
9. Little Sister ______ him food. eats (gives)
10. Little Critter gives him ______. (water) toys

**Consonant Digraphs (1-3):** Have your child name each picture, listen to the beginning sound, and write the beginning consonant digraph in the blank below the picture.
**Long Vowels (4-6):** Have your child name each picture and listen to the vowel sound, then write the letters that complete the picture name.
**Facts and Details (7-10):** Have your child read each sentence and, based on the story events, circle the correct answer.

53

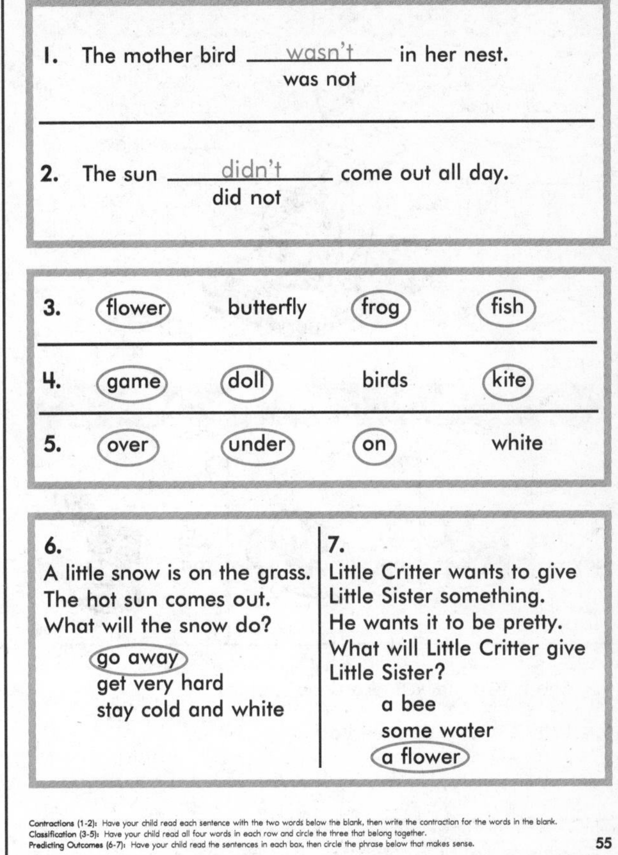

1. The mother bird wasn't in her nest.
   was not
2. The sun didn't come out all day.
   did not

3. (flower) butterfly (frog) (fish)
4. (game) (doll) birds (kite)
5. (over) (under) (on) white

6. A little snow is on the grass. The hot sun comes out. What will the snow do?
   - (go away)
   - get very hard
   - stay cold and white

7. Little Critter wants to give Little Sister something. He wants it to be pretty. What will Little Critter give Little Sister?
   - a bee
   - some water
   - (a flower)

**Contractions (1-2):** Have your child read each sentence with the two words below the blank, then write the contraction for the words in the blank.
**Classification (3-5):** Have your child read all four words in each row and circle the three that belong together.
**Predicting Outcomes (6-7):** Have your child read the sentences in each box, then circle the phrase below that makes sense.

55

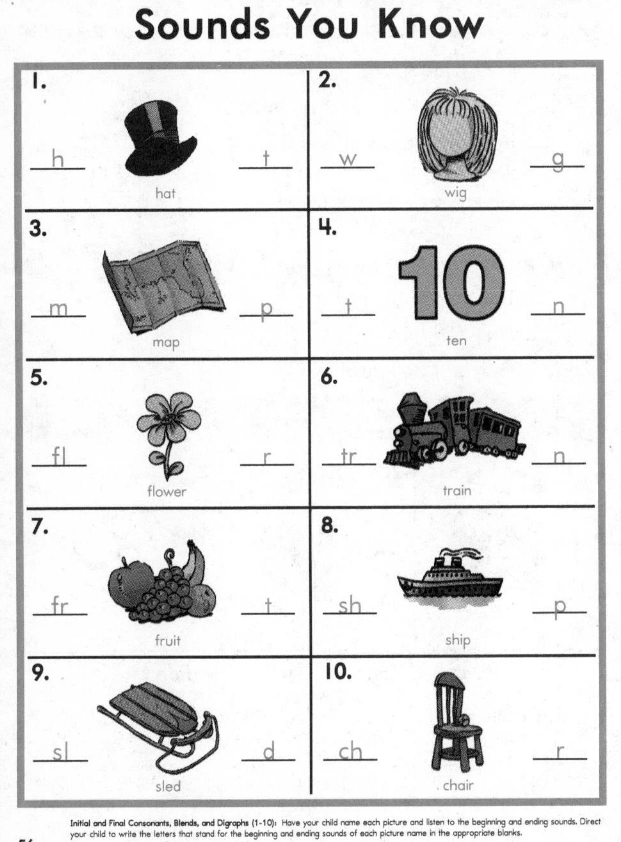

## Sounds You Know

1. h hat t
2. w wig g
3. m map p
4. t ten n
5. fl flower r
6. tr train n
7. fr fruit t
8. sh ship p
9. sl sled d
10. ch chair r

**Initial and Final Consonants, Blends, and Digraphs (1-10):** Have your child name each picture and listen to the beginning and ending sounds. Direct your child to write the letters that stand for the beginning and ending sounds of each picture name in the appropriate blanks.

56

## Words You Know

1. run (sun) fun
2. friend faster (flower)
3. big (birds) ball
4. (dog) did don't
5. (pond) play day
6. (puppy) cup sun
7. to too (two)
8. (fish) frog butterfly
9. go (game) give
10. (hot) not now
11. goes (grass) good
12. (three) there them
13. yellow (yard) yes
14. be big (bee)
15. could come (cold)

**Word Recognition (1-15):** Have your child name each picture and circle the word that names or best describes the picture.

57

## Reading and Thinking

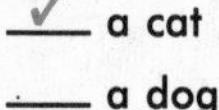

1. This story is about
   ___ school
   ✓ a cat
   ___ a dog

2. The cat has
   ___ a mouse
   ___ stripes
   ✓ spots

## Working with Words

1. (play) day 

2. cat (hat) 

3. 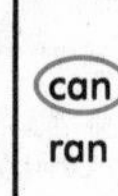 (can) ran 

4. She h_a_d black and orange spots.
5. Little Critter j_u_mped back.

**Reading and Thinking** Main Idea (1): Have your child complete the sentence by writing a check beside the correct answer. Picture Clues (2): Have your child look at the picture and complete the sentence by writing a check beside the correct answer.
**Working with Words** Initial Consonants (1-3): Have your child name each picture and circle the word that names it. Short Vowels (4-5): Have your child read each sentence, then complete each unfinished word by writing the missing vowel.

59

## Reading and Thinking

1. Little Critter did not see the ___.
   ___ hat
   ✓ cat
   ___ home

2. Where is Little Critter going?
   ___ out to play
   ___ on a bus
   ✓ to school

## Working with Words

1.  c_a_t

2. 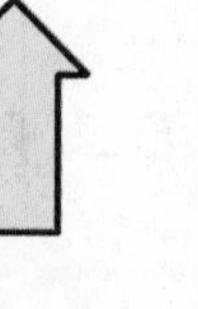 _u_p 

3.  L_i_ttle Cr_i_tter

not race kiss meet

4. feet ___meet___
5. got ___not___
6. face ___race___
7. miss ___kiss___

**Reading and Thinking** Drawing Conclusions (1): Have your child complete the sentence by writing a check beside the correct answer. Predicting Outcomes (2): Have your child read the question and, based on the story events, write a check beside the correct answer.
**Working with Words** Short Vowels (1-3): Have your child name each picture, listen to the vowel sound, and write the vowel that completes the picture name. Rhyming Words (4-7): Have your child read the words at the top of the exercise, then read each numbered word. Ask your child to find the word at the top that rhymes with the numbered word, then write the rhyming word in the blank.

61

## Reading and Thinking

1. Why was the cat at school?
   ___ Miss Kitty brought it.
   ✓ She followed Little Critter.
   ___ The cat was hungry.
2. What did the cat do to Miss Kitty?
   The cat rubbed against
   Miss Kitty.

## Working with Words

1. The ___cat___ is Little Critter's friend.
   cat bat
2. Let's read a good ___book___.
   book look

| | | | |
|---|---|---|---|
| 3. just | don't | school | (must) |
| 4. him | (Jim) | boy | they |
| 5. could | bed | desk | (would) |

**Reading and Thinking** Cause and Effect (1): Have your child read the question and write a check beside the correct answer. Facts and Details (2): Have your child read the question and write the answer in the blanks.
**Working with Words** Initial Consonants (1-2): Have your child read each sentence and write the word that best completes it. Rhyming Words (3-5): Have your child read the words in each row. Ask your child to circle the word that rhymes with the first word in each row.

63

## Reading and Thinking

1. This story is about
   ___ how Miss Kitty teaches Math.
   ✓ how the class will find the cat's owner.
   ___ Little Critter's desk at school.
2. What did the class do to help the cat?
   ✓ They made signs.
   ___ They fed her.
   ___ They put her outside.

## Working with Words

1. (bus) but 

2. can (cat)  

3.  had (hat)  

don't can't let's didn't

4. can not ___can't___
5. do not ___don't___
6. did not ___didn't___
7. let us ___let's___

**Reading and Thinking** Main Idea (1): Have your child complete the sentence by writing a check beside the correct answer. Drawing Conclusions (2): Have your child read the question and write a check beside the correct answer.
**Working with Words** Final Consonants (1-3): Have your child name each picture and circle the word that names it. Contractions (4-7): Have your child read the contractions at the top of the exercise, then read each numbered pair of words. Have your child write the contraction for the two words in the blank.

65

## Reading and Thinking

1. Where did the class put signs?
   The class put signs in the hardware store and the toy store.

2. Why did Little Critter want to find another spot for his sign?
   ✓ He was afraid of Puddles.
   ___ Mr. Rubble was mean.
   ___ He didn't see a door.

## Working with Words

| 1. | 2. | 3. |
|---|---|---|
|   |  | 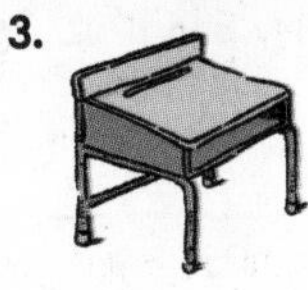 |
| sh_o_p | M_o_lly | d_e_sk |

4. (ask)ed (ask)ing — ask
5. (walk)s (walk)ed — walk
6. (bark)s (bark)ing — bark

**Reading and Thinking** Facts and Details (1): Have your child read the question and write the answer in the blank. Drawing Conclusions (2): Have your child read the question and write a check beside the correct answer.
**Working with Words** Short Vowels (1-3): Have your child name each picture, listen to the vowel sound, and write the vowel that completes the picture name. Base Words and Endings (4-6): Have your child read the words, circle the base words, and write each base word in the blank.



## Reading and Thinking

1.
   3 Little Sister asked to keep the kittens.
   2 There were eight cats in the clubhouse.
   1 They looked in the clubhouse.

2. The mother cat had kittens.
   mother must

3. There were eight cats.
   egg eight

## Working with Words

| 1. | 2. | 3. |
|---|---|---|
|  |  |  |
| m_other | k_ittens | h_ouse |

| 4. | 5. | 6. |
|---|---|---|
| (glass) grass 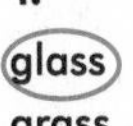 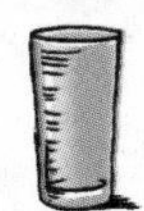 | desk (drink)   | (sleep) stop   |

**Reading and Thinking** Sequence (1): Have your child read the sentences and number them to show the order of events in the story. Context Clues (2-3): Have your child read each sentence and write the word that best completes it.
**Working with Words** Initial Consonants (1-3): Have your child name each picture, listen to the beginning sound, and write the letter that completes the picture name. Blends (4-6): Have your child name each picture and circle the word that names or best describes it.



## Reading and Thinking

1. We took the puppy for a walk.
   wall walk

2. The boy threw the ball to his friend.
   their threw

3. Don't throw that string away.
   those throw

## Working with Words

| 1. | 2. | 3. |
|---|---|---|
| (three) throw  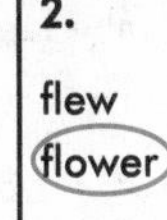 | flew (flower)  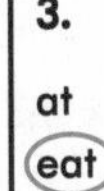 | at (eat)  |

## Learning to Study

1. ecd c d e
2. hgf f g h
3. pon n o p
4. srt r s t

**Reading and Thinking** Context Clues (1-3): Have your child read each sentence and write the word that best completes it.
**Working with Words** Vowel Digraphs and Dipthongs (1-3): Have your child name each picture and circle the word that names or best describes it. Learning to Study Alphabetical Order (1-4): Have your child write each set of letters in alphabetical order.



## Reading and Thinking

1. This story takes place at
   ___ school. ✓ the market. ___ the farm.

2. Why did Mr. Molini need a cat?
   ___ He needed someone to walk with.
   ___ He needed someone to watch the store.
   ✓ He wanted a cat to chase mice.

## Working with Words

| 1. | 2. | 3. |
|---|---|---|
|  |   |  |
| r_o_s_e | b_i_t_e | m_u_l_e |

1. Do you know where she lives?
   there where

2. Is that your cat over there?
   that what

**Reading and Thinking** Drawing Conclusions (1): Have your child complete the sentence by writing a check beside the correct answer. Cause and Effect (2): Have your child read the question and write a check beside the correct answer.
**Working with Words** Long Vowels (1-3): Have your child name each picture, listen to the vowel sound, and write the letters that complete the picture name. Consonant Digraphs (4-5): Have your child read each sentence and write the word that best completes it.

## Reading and Thinking

1. This story is about
   ___ feeding the kittens.
   ___ cleaning the house.
   _✓_ baking a cake.

2. Little Critter wanted to
   ___ run. ___ play. _✓_ help.

## Working with Words

1. Can your pet do a _tr_ick?
2. Who _cl_osed the window?
3. A farm is a _pl_ace for animals.

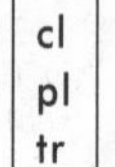

cl
pl
tr

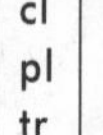

---

4. The boy's cat ___sleeps___ on his bed.
   sleeps sleeping
5. I ___looked___ at the funny picture.
   looks looked
6. He is ___showing___ the children a book.
   showed showing

**Reading and Thinking** Main Idea (1): Have your child complete the sentence by writing a check beside the correct answer. Drawing Conclusions (2): Have your child complete the sentence by writing a check beside the correct answer.
**Working with Words** Blends(1-3): Have your child read each sentence and look at the blends in the small box, then complete each unfinished word by writing the missing blend. Base Words and Endings (4-6): Have your child read each sentence and write the word that correctly completes it.

75

## Reading and Thinking

1. What was Mr. Critter doing in the yard?
   ___ He was planting flowers.
   _✓_ He was planting a tree.
   ___ He was cutting the grass.

2. When I ___cover___ my eyes, I can't see.
   could cover
3. The funny kittens ___climb___ the tree.
   climb chose

## Working with Words

1. My bed h_a_s three covers on it.
2. He g_o_t a balloon at the circus.

---

ball balls top tops

3.  ___top___
4.  ___balls___
5.  ___tops___
6.  ___ball___

**Reading and Thinking** Drawing Conclusions (1): Have your child read the question and write a check beside the correct answer. Context Clues (2-3): Have your child read each sentence and write the word that best completes it.
**Working with Words** Short Vowels (1-2): Have your child read each sentence, then complete each unfinished word by writing the missing vowel. Singular and Plural (3-6): Have your child read the words at the top of the exercise. Ask your child to look at each picture and, in the blank, write the word that names it.

77

## Reading and Thinking

1. 1 2 3
   _1_ Malcolm wanted to meet Little Critter.
   _3_ Little Critter told Malcolm to come any time.
   _2_ Malcolm petted a kitten.
2. Why can't Malcolm have a cat?
   _✓_ They make his mother sneeze.
   ___ Cats sneeze a lot.
   ___ He doesn't like cats.

## Working with Words

1. Grandma told ___us___ a story.
   up us
2. We gave ___them___ some flowers.
   then them

---

| | | | | |
|---|---|---|---|---|
| 3. | **met** | much | desk | (pet) |
| 4. | **pick** | why | (sick) | Molly |
| 5. | **came** | rose | (name) | come |
| 6. | **walk** | little | way | (talk) |

**Reading and Thinking** Sequence (1): Have your child read the sentences and number them to show the order of events in the story. Facts and Details (2): Have your child read the question and write a check beside the correct answer.
**Working with Words** Final Consonants (1-2): Have your child read each sentence and write the word that best completes it. Rhyming Words (3-6): Have your child read the words in each row, then circle the word that rhymes with the first word in each row.

79

## Reading and Thinking

1. Who did Little Critter talk to at the zoo?
   Little Critter talked to Ms. Dingo.
2. What animal did Little Critter see at the zoo?
   ___ a kitten
   _✓_ a tiger
   ___ a lion

## Working with Words

1. _Wh_en she saw the surprise, she laughed.
2. _Sh_e threw the ball to me.
3. _Th_ank you for helping us.
4. _Th_is has been a good day.

Sh
Th
Wh

---

5. When I called the cat, it c_a_m_e_.
6. He m_a_d_e_ a new friend at school.
7. H_e_ can't find his new hat.
8. Do you l_i_k_e_ to eat apples?

**Reading and Thinking** Facts and Details (1): Have your child read the question and write the answer in the blank. Drawing Conclusions (2): Have your child read the question and write a check beside the correct answer.
**Working with Words** Consonant Digraphs (1-4): Have your child read each sentence and look at the consonant digraphs in the small box. Have your child complete each unfinished word by writing the missing consonant digraph. One of the consonant digraphs will be used twice. Long Vowels (5-8): Have your child read each sentence, then complete each unfinished word by writing the missing letters.

81

## Reading and Thinking

1. Which is not a good place for cats?

   ____ at home ____ in the yard ✓ Stork's Toy Shop

2. I __hope__ you will like the surprise.

   happy hope

3. There is glass in the __window__.

   without window

## Working with Words

1. three (tree)
2. (flowers) found
3. sleep (stop)

4. I have two __cats__ for pets.
5. The brown __cat__ likes to play.
6. One time it got stuck in a __tree__.
7. The other cat does not like __trees__.

cat
cats
tree
trees

Reading and Thinking Picture Clues (1): Have your child look at the picture that accompanies the story, then complete the unfinished sentence by writing a check beside the correct answer. Context Clues (2-3): Have your child read each sentence and write the word that best completes it. Working with Words Blends (1-3): Have your child name each picture and circle the word that names or best describes it. Singular and Plural (4-7): Have your child read the sentences and the words in the small box, then choose the word that makes sense in each sentence and write it in the blank.

83

## Reading and Thinking

1. Why didn't Rusty keep a kitten?

   ____ He is afraid of cats.

   ____ Cats make him sneeze.

   ✓ His repair shop was not safe for kittens.

AUTO REPAIR

2. This story is about

   ✓ the Auto Repair Shop. ____ the zoo.

   ____ the wagon.

## Working with Words

1. think (trick)
2. (fly) from
3. sleep (stuck)

4. We saw a good __show__ about a dog.

   know show

5. Are these your __things__?

   things time

6. __Where__ is the man's house?

   Where Wish

Reading and Thinking Cause and Effect (1): Have your child read the question and write a check beside the correct answer. Main Idea (2): Have your child complete the sentence by writing a check beside the correct answer.
Working with Words Blends (1-3): Have your child name each picture and circle the word that names or best describes it. Consonant Digraphs (4-6): Have your child read each sentence and write the word that best completes it.

85

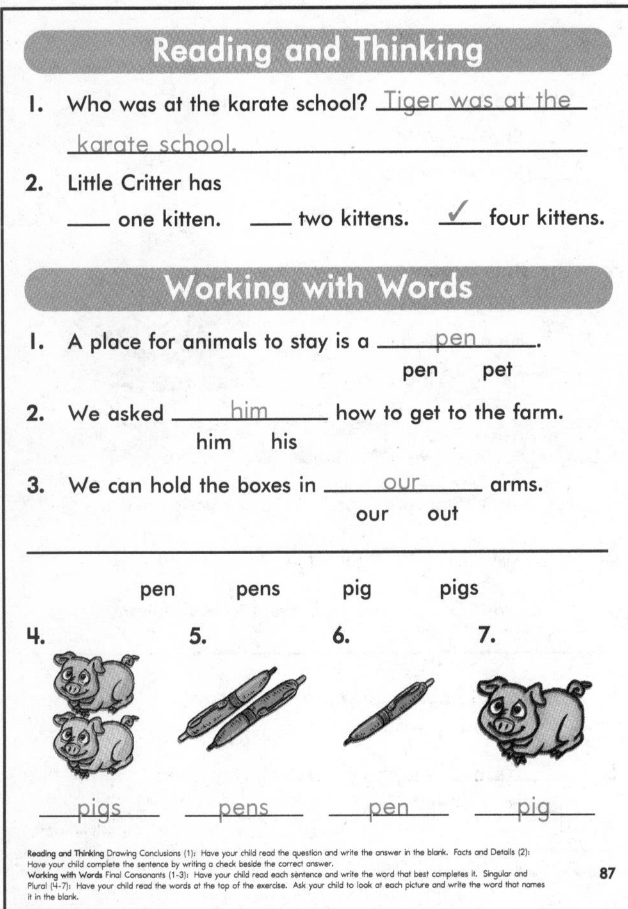

## Reading and Thinking

1. Who was at the karate school? __Tiger was at the karate school.__
2. Little Critter has

   ____ one kitten. ____ two kittens. ✓ four kittens.

## Working with Words

1. A place for animals to stay is a __pen__.

   pen pet

2. We asked __him__ how to get to the farm.

   him his

3. We can hold the boxes in __our__ arms.

   our out

pen pens pig pigs

4. __pigs__
5. __pens__
6. __pen__
7. __pig__

Reading and Thinking Drawing Conclusions (1): Have your child read the question and write the answer in the blank. Facts and Details (2): Have your child complete the sentence by writing a check beside the correct answer.
Working with Words Final Consonants (1-3): Have your child read each sentence and write the word that best completes it. Singular and Plural (4-7): Have your child read the words at the top of the exercise. Ask your child to look at each picture and write the word that names it in the blank.

87

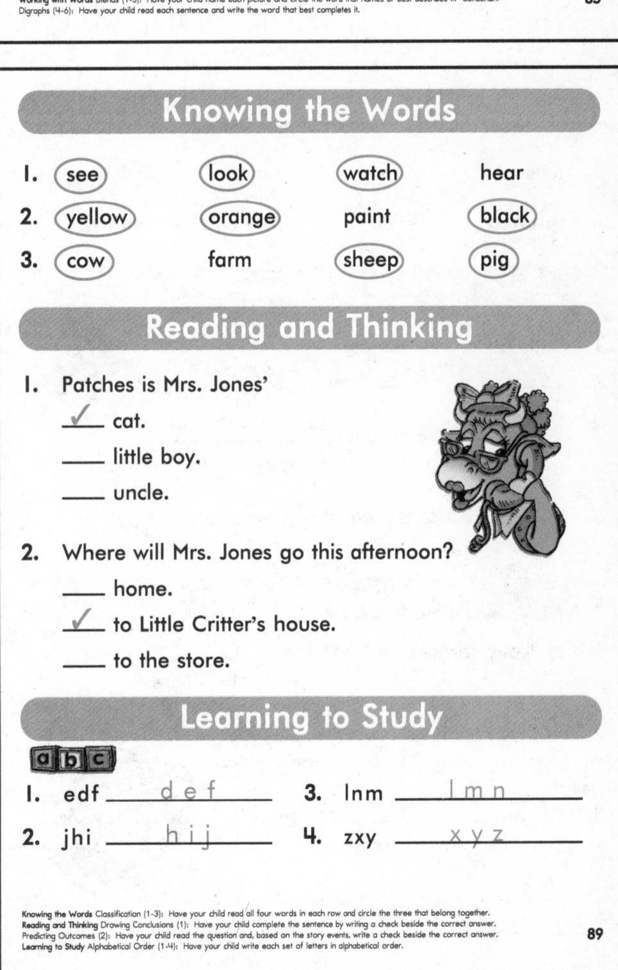

## Knowing the Words

1. (see) (look) (watch) hear
2. (yellow) (orange) paint (black)
3. (cow) farm (sheep) (pig)

## Reading and Thinking

1. Patches is Mrs. Jones'

   ✓ cat.

   ____ little boy.

   ____ uncle.

2. Where will Mrs. Jones go this afternoon?

   ____ home.

   ✓ to Little Critter's house.

   ____ to the store.

## Learning to Study

abc

1. edf __d e f__
2. jhi __h i j__
3. lnm __l m n__
4. zxy __x y z__

Knowing the Words Classification (1-3): Have your child read all four words in each row and circle the three that belong together.
Reading and Thinking Drawing Conclusions (1): Have your child complete the sentence by writing a check beside the correct answer.
Predicting Outcomes (2): Have your child read the question and, based on the story events, write a check beside the correct answer.
Learning to Study Alphabetical Order (1-4): Have your child write each set of letters in alphabetical order.

89

## Reading and Thinking

1. Little Sister was having a
   ___ game. ✓ party. ___ meal.

2. What was the mother cat wearing?
   ___ a collar
   ___ socks
   ✓ a dress

## Working with Words

1. (pout) shout

2. (dress) drink

3. (cup) cry

4. We saw two kittens at the farm.
5. The kittens had brown tails.
6. One kitten was just a baby.
7. Its tail was not very long.

kitten
kittens
tail
tails

**Reading and Thinking** Picture Clues (1): Have your child look at the picture that accompanies the story, then complete the unfinished sentence by writing a check beside the correct answer. Predicting Outcomes (2): Have your child read the question and, based on the story events, write a check beside the correct answer.
**Working with Words** Consonant Digraphs (1-3): Have your child name each picture and circle the word that names or best describes it. Singular and Plural (4-7): Have your child read the sentences and the words in the small box, then choose the word that makes sense in each sentence, and write it in the blank.

91

## Reading and Thinking

1. Look at the story picture. Patches' fur was
   ___ black. ___ orange. ✓ black and orange.

2. 2 Mrs. Critter was glad to find Patches' owner.
   3 Mrs. Jones said thank you.
   1 Mrs. Jones came over.

3. His dog got a prize at the pet show.
   play prize right

4. Dad helped me onto the horse.
   into only onto

## Working with Words

1. (farm) frog

2. glad (glass)

3. (tail) tell

I'll that's let's don't

4. that is that's
5. I will I'll
6. let us let's
7. do not don't

**Reading and Thinking** Picture Clues (1): Have your child look at the picture that accompanies the story, then complete the unfinished sentence by writing a check beside the correct answer. Sequence (2): Have your child read the sentences and number them to show the order of events in the story. Context Clues (3-4): Have your child read each sentence and write the word that best completes it.
**Working with Words** Vowel Digraphs and Diphthongs (1-3): Have your child name each picture and circle the word that names or best describes it. Contractions (4-7): Have your child read the contractions at the top of the exercise, then read each numbered pair of words. Have your child write the contraction for the two words in the blank.

93

## Knowing the Words

1. (eyes) (ears) think (nose)

2. (grumpy) little (unhappy) (angry)

## Reading and Thinking

1. Little Sister was feeling
   ✓ sad. ___ happy. ___ angry.

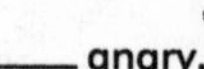

2. We are going to the farm today.
   today told turned

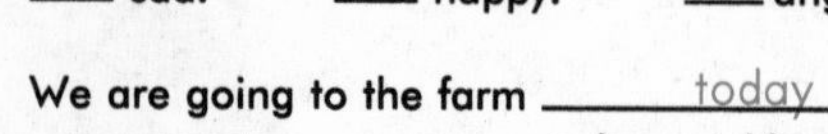

3. A lion would not make a good pet.
   cat dog lion

## Working with Words

1. Malcolm threw a ball into the air.
   air are

2. Will you read us a story now?
   new now

3. Do you see the circus?
   saw see

**Knowing the Words** Classification (1-2): Have your child read all four words in each row and circle the three that belong together.
**Reading and Thinking** Facts and Details (1): Have your child complete the sentence by writing a check beside the correct answer. Context Clues (2-3): Have your child read each sentence and write the word that best completes it.
**Working with Words** Vowel Digraphs and Diphthongs (1-3): Have your child read each sentence and write the word that best completes it.

95

## Reading and Thinking

1. Why did Little Sister hide with the kittens?
   ___ She was cold.
   ✓ She wanted to keep the kittens.
   ___ The kittens were playing.

2. This story is about
   ✓ hiding in the closet.
   ___ running away.
   ___ going to the zoo.

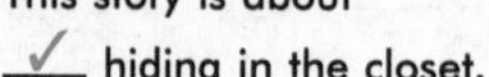

## Working with Words

1. I h o p e you get a pr i z e for your picture.
2. H e asked me to let him r i d e the horse.
3. W e will t a k e some flowers to Mr. Molini.

4. I am wishing you a happy day.
   wished wishing
5. I pulled the covers over my head.
   pulls pulled

**Reading and Thinking** Drawing Conclusions (1): Have your child read the question and write a check beside the correct answer. Main Idea (2): Have your child complete the sentence by writing a check beside the correct answer.
**Working with Words** Long Vowels (1-3): Have your child read each sentence, then complete each unfinished word by writing the missing letters. Base Words and Endings (4-5): Have your child read each sentence and write the word that correctly completes it.

97

## Knowing the Words

1. **jumping** **throwing** sleep **running**
2. **words** **story** **book** box
3. maybe **Mr.** **Ms.** **Mrs.**
4. **shoulder** **head** **arm** car

## Reading and Thinking

1. This story takes place in the
   ___ farm. ___ zoo. _✓_ car.
2. Who was not in the car with Little Critter?
   ___ Little Sister. ___ Mrs. Critter. _✓_ Grandma

## Learning to Study

1. car arm box
   _arm_
   _box_
   _car_

2. kitten little jump
   _jump_
   _kitten_
   _little_

Knowing the Words Classification (1-4): Have your child read all four words in each row and circle the three that belong together.
Reading and Thinking Drawing Conclusions (1): Have your child complete the sentence by writing a check beside the correct answer. Facts and Details (2): Have your child read the question and write a check beside the correct answer.
Learning to Study Alphabetical Order (1-2): Have your child read each set of words and write them in alphabetical order.

99

## Reading and Thinking

1. Where did the kitten go?
   ___ into the house.
   _✓_ into the barn.
   ___ under the fence.

2. Mr. Critter _found_ some money in his pocket.
   found friend
3. The man likes to read _while_ he eats lunch.
   while will

## Working with Words

| |
|---|
| ch |
| sh |
| th |
| wh |

1. She will _sh_ow the dog a new trick.
2. I watched their baby _wh_ile they were gone.
3. _Th_ose _ch_ildren go to my school.

4. _I'll_ buy a balloon for Malcolm.
   I will
5. We _didn't_ make it to the bus stop on time.
   did not

Reading and Thinking Predicting Outcomes (1): Have your child read the question and based on the story events, write a check beside the correct answer. Context Clues (2-3): Have your child read each sentence and write the word that best completes it.
Working with Words Consonant Digraphs (1-3): Have your child read each sentence, then complete each unfinished word by writing the missing letters. Point out that sentence 3 should begin with a capital letter. Contractions (4-5): Have your child read each sentence with the two words below the blank. In the blank, have your child write the contraction for the words.

101

## Reading and Thinking

1. _3_ Little Critter fell asleep.
   _2_ Little Critter went to the sheep barn.
   _1_ Little Critter went to the chicken coop.
2. This story is about
   ___ a funny sheep.
   _✓_ a place to nap.
   ___ a big lunch.

## Working with Words

1. H_e_ will w_a_k_e_ up soon.
2. A m_u_l_e_ looks a little l_i_k_e_ a horse.

3. A sheep _eats_ grass.
   eats eating
4. I laughed when Malcolm _tricked_ me.
   tricks tricked
5. I can hear Dad _calling_ me.
   called calling

Reading and Thinking Sequence (1): Have your child read the sentences and number them to show the order of events in the story. Main Idea (2): Have your child complete the sentence by writing a check beside the correct answer.
Working with Words Long Vowels (1-2): Have your child read each sentence, then complete each unfinished word by writing the missing letters. Base Words and Endings (3-5): Have your child read each sentence and write the word that correctly completes it.

103

## Reading and Thinking

1. Little Critter had
   ___ a big breakfast.
   _✓_ a fun day.
   ___ a bad dream.

2. Why did Little Critter want to surprise Little Sister?
   _Little Critter wanted to surprise Little Sister_
   _because she was sad._

## Working with Words

| 1. | 2. | 3. |
|---|---|---|
| c_a_t | g_e_t | c_a_n |
| f_a_t | l_e_t | f_a_n |
| h_a_t | w_e_t | m_a_n |

4. **read** ride

5. book **boxes**

6. **sneeze** snow

Reading and Thinking Facts and Details (1): Have your child complete the sentence by writing a check beside the correct answer. Cause and Effect (2): Have your child read the question and write the answer in the blanks.
Working with Words Short Vowels, Rhyming Words (1-3): Using the completed item as an example, have your child form rhyming words in each column by writing the same vowel in each blank. Vowel Digraphs and Diphthongs (4-6): Have your child name each picture and circle the word that names or best describes it.

105

## Knowing the Words

1. (flowers) (grass) boxes (tree)
2. (table) (bed) (desk) window
3. (boy) she (uncle) (man)

## Reading and Thinking

1. Who helped Little Critter surprise Little Sister?

   Grandma helped Little Critter.

2. Tangerine has ________ fur.

   ___ green ✓ orange ___ spotted

## Learning to Study

1. goat horse funny
2. rose table shoe

| 1. | 2. |
|---|---|
| funny | rose |
| goat | shoe |
| horse | table |

Knowing the Words Classification (1-3): Have your child read all four words in each row and circle the three that belong together.
Reading and Thinking Facts and Details (1): Have your child read the question and write the answer in the blank. Picture Clues (2): Have your child look at the picture that accompanies the story, then complete the unfinished sentence by writing a check beside the correct answer.
Learning to Study Alphabetical Order(1-2): Have your child read each set of words and write them in alphabetical order.

107

## Reading and Thinking

1. What did Little Critter do when he saw the dog?

   ___ He fell asleep.
   ✓ He opened the door.
   ___ He woke up Little Sister.

2. Do you think Little Critter will help the dog?

   ________ Why or why not? ________

   Answers will vary.

## Working with Words

1. Molly and I are in the s_a_m_e_ room at school.
2. I h_o_p_e_ Maurice will wr_i_t_e_ to me.
3. What t_i_m_e_ does the bus stop here?

4. can not can't
5. let us let's
6. that is that's
7. I will I'll

Reading and Thinking Facts and Details (1): Have your child read the question and write a check beside the correct answer. Predicting Outcomes (2): Have your child read the questions and, based on the story events and his or her own opinion, write the answers in the blanks.
Working with Words Long Vowels (1-3): Have your child read each sentence, then complete each unfinished word by writing the missing letters. Contractions (4-7): Have your child read the two words beside each blank. In the blank, have your child write the contraction for the words.

109

# SPECTRUM

## SPECTRUM WORKBOOKS ILLUSTRATED BY MERCER MAYER!

Grades K–2 • 128–160 full-color pages • Size: 8.375" x 10.875" • Paperback

McGraw-Hill, the premier educational publisher for grades PreK–12, and acclaimed children's author and illustrator, Mercer Mayer, are the proud creators of this workbook line featuring the lovable Little Critter. Like other Spectrum titles, the length, breadth, and depth of the activities in these workbooks enable children to learn a variety of skills about a single subject.

- Mercer Mayer's Little Critter family of characters has sold over 50 million books. These wholesome characters and stories appeal to both parents and teachers.
- Each full-color workbook is based on highly respected McGraw-Hill Companies' textbooks.
- All exercises feature easy-to-follow instructions.
- An answer key is included in each workbook.

| TITLE | ISBN | PRICE |
|---|---|---|
| **LANGUAGE ARTS** | | |
| Grade K | 1-57768-840-6 | $8.95 |
| Grade 1 | 1-57768-841-4 | $8.95 |
| Grade 2 | 1-57768-842-2 | $8.95 |
| **MATH** | | |
| Grade K | 1-57768-800-7 | $8.95 |
| Grade 1 | 1-57768-801-5 | $8.95 |
| Grade 2 | 1-57768-802-3 | $8.95 |
| **PHONICS** | | |
| Grade K | 1-57768-820-1 | $8.95 |
| Grade 1 | 1-57768-821-X | $8.95 |
| Grade 2 | 1-57768-822-8 | $8.95 |
| **READING** | | |
| Grade K | 1-57768-810-4 | $8.95 |
| Grade 1 | 1-57768-811-2 | $8.95 |
| Grade 2 | 1-57768-812-0 | $8.95 |
| **SPELLING** | | |
| Grade K | 1-57768-830-9 | $8.95 |
| Grade 1 | 1-57768-831-7 | $8.95 |
| Grade 2 | 1-57768-832-5 | $8.95 |
| **WRITING** | | |
| Grade K | 1-57768-850-3 | $8.95 |
| Grade 1 | 1-57768-851-1 | $8.95 |
| Grade 2 | 1-57768-852-X | $8.95 |

Prices subject to change without notice.

Wholesome, well-known characters plus proven school curriculum equals learning success!

## Coming in June 2003!

| TITLE | ISBN | PRICE |
|---|---|---|
| **PRESCHOOL** | | |
| Basic Concepts | 1-57768-509-1 | $8.95 |
| Letters and Sounds | 1-57768-539-3 | $8.95 |
| Numbers and Counting | 1-57768-519-9 | $8.95 |
| Reading Readiness | 1-57768-529-6 | $8.95 |
| Beginning Math | 1-57768-579-2 | $8.95 |
| Beginning Phonics | 1-57768-589-X | $8.95 |
| Beginning Reading | 1-57768-599-7 | $8.95 |
| Beginning Writing | 1-57768-549-0 | $8.95 |

Prices subject to change without notice.

# SPECTRUM

Brought to you by McGraw-Hill, the premier educational publisher for grades PreK–12. All our workbooks meet school curriculum guidelines and correspond to The McGraw-Hill Companies' classroom textbooks.

## LANGUAGE ARTS

Grades 3–6 • 160 full-color pages
Size: 8.375" x 10.875" • Paperback

Encourages creativity and builds confidence by making writing fun! Sixty four-part lessons strengthen writing skills by focusing on parts of speech, word usage, sentence structure, punctuation, and proofreading. This series is based on the highly respected SRA/McGraw-Hill language arts series. Answer key included.

## MATH

Grades K–8 • Over 150 pages
Size: 8.375" x 10.875" • Paperback

Features easy-to-follow instructions that give students a clear path to success. This series includes comprehensive coverage of the basic skills, helping children master math fundamentals. Answer key included.

## PHONICS/WORD STUDY

Grades K–6 • Over 200 pages
Size: 8.375" x 10.875" • Paperback

Provides everything children need to build multiple skills in language arts. This series focuses on phonics, structural analysis, and dictionary skills, and offers creative ideas for using phonics and word study skills in language areas. Answer key included.

| TITLE | ISBN | PRICE |
|---|---|---|
| **LANGUAGE ARTS** | | |
| Gr. 3 | 1-57768-483-4 | $8.95 |
| Gr. 4 | 1-57768-484-2 | $8.95 |
| Gr. 5 | 1-57768-485-0 | $8.95 |
| Gr. 6 | 1-57768-486-9 | $8.95 |
| **MATH** | | |
| Gr. K | 1-57768-400-1 | $8.95 |
| Gr. 1 | 1-57768-401-X | $8.95 |
| Gr. 2 | 1-57768-402-8 | $8.95 |
| Gr. 3 | 1-57768-403-6 | $8.95 |
| Gr. 4 | 1-57768-404-4 | $8.95 |
| Gr. 5 | 1-57768-405-2 | $8.95 |
| Gr. 6 | 1-57768-406-0 | $8.95 |
| Gr. 7 | 1-57768-407-9 | $8.95 |
| Gr. 8 | 1-57768-408-7 | $8.95 |
| **PHONICS (Grades K–3)/WORD STUDY and PHONICS (Grades 4–6)** | | |
| Gr. K | 1-57768-450-8 | $8.95 |
| Gr. 1 | 1-57768-451-6 | $8.95 |
| Gr. 2 | 1-57768-452-4 | $8.95 |
| Gr. 3 | 1-57768-453-2 | $8.95 |
| Gr. 4 | 1-57768-454-0 | $8.95 |
| Gr. 5 | 1-57768-455-9 | $8.95 |
| Gr. 6 | 1-57768-456-7 | $8.95 |
| **READING** | | |
| Gr. K | 1-57768-460-5 | $8.95 |
| Gr. 1 | 1-57768-461-3 | $8.95 |
| Gr. 2 | 1-57768-462-1 | $8.95 |
| Gr. 3 | 1-57768-463-X | $8.95 |
| Gr. 4 | 1-57768-464-8 | $8.95 |
| Gr. 5 | 1-57768-465-6 | $8.95 |
| Gr. 6 | 1-57768-466-4 | $8.95 |

**Prices subject to change without notice.**

## READING

Grades K–6 • Over 150 full-color pages
Size: 8.375" x 10.875" • Paperback

This full-color series creates an enjoyable reading environment, even for below-average readers. Each book contains captivating content, colorful characters, and compelling illustrations, so children are eager to find out what happens next. Answer key included.

## SPELLING

Grades 3–6 • 160 full-color pages
Size: 8.375" x 10.875" • Paperback

This full-color series links spelling to reading and writing, and increases skills in words and meanings, consonant and vowel spellings, and proofreading practice. Speller dictionary and answer key included.

## VOCABULARY

Grades 3–6 • 160 full-color pages
Size: 8.375" x 10.875" • Paperback

An essential building block for writing and reading proficiency, this series extends vocabulary knowledge through grade-appropriate instruction and activities. Synonyms, antonyms, homophones, word families, and word forms are among the key concepts explored. Instruction is based on language arts and reading standards, offering a solid foundation for language arts, spelling, and reading comprehension. The series features a proficiency test practice section for standards-aligned assessment. Answer key included.

## WRITING

Grades 3–6 • 160 full-color pages
Size: 8.375" x 10.875" • Paperback

Lessons focus on creative and expository writing using clearly stated objectives and pre-writing exercises. Eight essential reading skills are applied. Activities include main idea, sequence, comparison, detail, fact and opinion, cause and effect, making a point, and point of view. Each book includes a Writer's Handbook that offers writing tips. Answer key included.

## TEST PREP

Grades 1–8 • 160 full-color pages
Size: 8.375" x 10.875" • Paperback

This series teaches the skills, strategies, and techniques necessary for students to succeed on any standardized test. Each book contains guidelines and advice for parents along with study tips for students. Grades 1 and 2 cover Reading, Language Arts, Writing, and Math. Grades 3 through 8 cover Reading, Language Arts, Writing, Math, Social Studies, and Science.

## FLASH CARDS

Card size: 3.0625" x 4.5625"

Flash cards provide children with one of the most effective ways to drill and practice fundamentals. The cards have large type, making it easy for young learners to read them. Each pack contains 50 flash cards, including a parent instruction card that offers suggestions for fun, creative activities and games that reinforce children's skills development.

| TITLE | ISBN | PRICE |
|---|---|---|
| **SPELLING** | | |
| Gr. 3 | 1-57768-493-1 | $8.95 |
| Gr. 4 | 1-57768-494-X | $8.95 |
| Gr. 5 | 1-57768-495-8 | $8.95 |
| Gr. 6 | 1-57768-496-6 | $8.95 |
| **VOCABULARY** | | |
| Gr. 3 | 1-57768-793-0 | $8.95 |
| Gr. 4 | 1-57768-794-9 | $8.95 |
| Gr. 5 | 1-57768-795-7 | $8.95 |
| Gr. 6 | 1-57768-796-5 | $8.95 |
| **WRITING** | | |
| Gr. 3 | 1-57768-913-5 | $8.95 |
| Gr. 4 | 1-57768-914-3 | $8.95 |
| Gr. 5 | 1-57768-915-1 | $8.95 |
| Gr. 6 | 1-57768-916-X | $8.95 |
| **TEST PREP** | | |
| Gr. 1–2 | 1-57768-662-4 | $9.95 |
| Gr. 3 | 1-57768-663-2 | $9.95 |
| Gr. 4 | 1-57768-664-0 | $9.95 |
| Gr. 5 | 1-57768-665-9 | $9.95 |
| Gr. 6 | 1-57768-666-7 | $9.95 |
| Gr. 7 | 1-57768-667-5 | $9.95 |
| Gr. 8 | 1-57768-668-3 | $9.95 |
| **FLASH CARDS** | | |
| Addition | 1-57768-167-3 | $2.99 |
| Alphabet | 1-57768-151-7 | $2.99 |
| Division | 1-57768-158-4 | $2.99 |
| Money | 1-57768-150-9 | $2.99 |
| Multiplication | 1-57768-157-6 | $2.99 |
| Numbers | 1-57768-127-4 | $2.99 |
| Phonics | 1-57768-152-5 | $2.99 |
| Sight Words | 1-57768-160-6 | $2.99 |
| Subtraction | 1-57768-168-1 | $2.99 |
| Telling Time | 1-57768-138-X | $2.99 |

**Prices subject to change without notice.**

# FIRST READERS

The only first reader series based on school curriculum.

## MERCER MAYER FIRST READERS
## SKILLS AND PRACTICE

Levels 1, 2, 3 (Grades PreK–2) • 24 Pages • Size: 6" x 9" • Paperback

Young readers will enjoy these simple and engaging stories written with their reading level in mind. Featuring Mercer Mayer's charming illustrations and favorite Little Critter characters, these are the books children will want to read again and again. To ensure reading success, the First Readers are based on McGraw-Hill's respected educational SRA Open Court Reading Program. Skill-based activities in the back of the book also help reinforce learning. A word list is included for vocabulary practice. Each book contains 24 full-color pages.

**Level 1 (Grades PreK–K)**

| TITLE | ISBN | PRICE |
|---|---|---|
| Camping Out | 1-57768-806-6 | $3.95 |
| No One Can Play | 1-57768-804-X | $3.95 |
| Play Ball | 1-57768-803-1 | $3.95 |
| Snow Day | 1-57768-805-8 | $3.95 |
| Little Critter Slipcase 1 (Contains 4 titles; 1 each of the above titles) | 1-57768-823-6 | $15.95 |
| Show and Tell | 1-57768-835-X | $3.95 |
| New Kid in Town | 1-57768-829-5 | $3.95 |
| Country Fair | 1-57768-827-9 | $3.95 |
| My Trip to the Zoo | 1-57768-826-0 | $3.95 |
| Little Critter Slipcase 2 (Contains 4 titles; 1 each of the above titles) | 1-57768-853-8 | $15.95 |

**Level 2 (Grades K–1)**

| TITLE | ISBN | PRICE |
|---|---|---|
| The Mixed-Up Morning | 1-57768-808-2 | $3.95 |
| A Yummy Lunch | 1-57768-809-0 | $3.95 |
| Our Park | 1-57768-807-4 | $3.95 |
| Field Day | 1-57768-813-9 | $3.95 |
| Little Critter Slipcase 1 (Contains 4 titles; 1 each of the above titles) | 1-57768-824-4 | $15.95 |
| Beach Day | 1-57768-844-9 | $3.95 |
| The New Fire Truck | 1-57768-843-0 | $3.95 |
| A Day at Camp | 1-57768-836-8 | $3.95 |
| Tiger's Birthday | 1-57768-828-7 | $3.95 |
| Little Critter Slipcase 2 (Contains 4 titles; 1 each of the above titles) | 1-57768-854-6 | $15.95 |

**Level 3 (Grades 1–2)**

| TITLE | ISBN | PRICE |
|---|---|---|
| Surprise! | 1-57768-814-7 | $3.95 |
| Our Friend Sam | 1-57768-815-5 | $3.95 |
| Helping Mom | 1-57768-816-3 | $3.95 |
| My Trip to the Farm | 1-57768-817-1 | $3.95 |
| Little Critter Slipcase 1 (Contains 4 titles; 1 each of the above titles) | 1-57768-825-2 | $15.95 |
| Grandma's Garden | 1-57768-846-5 | $3.95 |
| Class Trip | 1-57768-845-7 | $3.95 |
| Goodnight, Little Critter | 1-57768-834-1 | $3.95 |
| Our Tree House | 1-57768-833-3 | $3.95 |
| Little Critter Slipcase 2 (Contains 4 titles; 1 each of the above titles) | 1-57768-855-4 | $15.95 |

**Prices subject to change without notice.**

The Children's Book Council has named **Snow Day** and **Our Friend Sam** recipients of the Council's "Children's Choices 2002" awards, placing the two titles among the highest recommended books for children.